THE SOUL
OF SUCCESS

Other titles by Bell:

Victory of the Spirit: Meditations on Black Quotations
Famous Black Quotations

THE SOUL
OF SUCCESS

Inspiring Quotations
for Entrepreneurs

JANET CHEATHAM BELL

John Wiley & Sons, Inc.
New York · Chichester · Weinheim · Brisbane · Singapore · Toronto

ISBN 0-471-18022-X

Printed in the United States of America
10 9 8 7 6 5 4 3 2 1

*Kamau, this book is for you
and the other young comedians
who are on their way
to phenomenal success.*

Contents

Foreword

As a college professor I admire good teaching. As an author I admire writers who, with a single stroke of their pen, capture and uplift the hearts of their readers. Janet Cheatham Bell knows the power of words. She knows that words unify and words break. Words heal and words destroy. Words bless us and words curse us. Most importantly, words encourage us and enlarge our spirit. In her own inimitable way, Janet continues to shape our lives.

There has never been a time when people were more desperately in need of faith and hope, of courage and peace of mind, of standards and ideals by which to live. There has never been a time when the tried and true beliefs and ideals of the past were more urgently needed to give each of us perspective and understanding—something on which to build the strong, firm foundation of our lives.

Today, society stands at the crossroads of human development. We are heirs of all that humanity has ever imagined and created—all that our forebears have ever written and expressed. Today, when we face life's most difficult challenges, when so many of us are troubled, uncertain, and confused, the words of wisdom offered to us by ours and previous generations take on a new and vital importance.

But where in the staggering wealth of ideas that has been passed down throughout the ages can we find the guidance that we desperately need? Where, in the thousands upon thousands of books and essays that transmit the best and brightest that mankind has to offer, can we find the inspiration that means the most? *The Soul of Success* is a combination of the most profound thoughts of some of the world's greatest achievers. Once again, we are given words—words that embolden and help us with future conquests— plain old common sense and unique insight into what motivates us to great achievement. It is singularly Janet Cheatham Bell.

I hope that you will enjoy this wonderful collection of quotations from some of the great men and women of our time. They are yours to read and enjoy, and to help light the way in your own life.

Dennis Kimbro

Acknowledgments

Thanks to my support team:
Arlene Williams, Madeline Scales-Taylor, Alvin
Foster, Almeda McPherson, Donn Nettles, Joy
Bergl, and my son Kamau. I couldn't have done it
without you. And to Carole Hall, because we
finally did it!

When You're Feeling Discontented

With their meager ambition to succeed where success was assured, they crowded the uncreative highway to the good job, the good wife, the good life. . . . They had no hunger, no goad of discontent.

Dorothy West

The emphasis in our education focused on preparing us for professional occupations rather than developing independent businesses as my grandfather had done.

Andrew Young

Those big checks are very seductive. As artists, we've been more concerned about getting a good job rather than having a business that provides jobs.

Warrington Hudlin

When times are tough, you can't afford to wait for someone to provide a job. You have to create your own by identifying a need and developing— or honing—the skills to fulfill that need.

Michelle Stevens

I wasn't doing what I was supposed to be doing. I knew that if I remained I would become a part of the system, and I knew that system was wrong.

Iyanla Vanzant

I remember a point in my life when I was afraid to dream. I didn't believe that I could change anything. I kept getting laid off, and I had to do something.

Ella L. J. Edmondson Bell

Today's workers are either getting a new lease on life or paying off the old one.

Michael Pellecchia

It's easy to work for somebody else; all you have to do is show up.

Rita Warford

All of my high-paying, high visibility corporate jobs had been high-anxiety.

George Fraser

I realized I was accustomed to corporate level pay and benefits, but not to job satisfaction.

Linda Shepard

It's important to stay committed and keep doing your job well, but use free time to pursue your dream. . . . You'll know when it's time to leave.

Terrie Williams

The return from your work must be the satisfaction which that work brings you. . . . With work which you despise, which bores you . . . this life is hell.

W. E. B. DuBois

If you don't love what you do, you'll never be successful at it.

Brian Tracy

Pain is the megaphone that calls us to change.

Marilyn Marcus

The changes in your life aren't always the ones you hoped for. But they can usually help you grow.

Pat Riley

Nothing anchors us to our pain other than fear.

Susan L. Taylor

My theory has always been that whatever the people who have all the money don't want you to do, that's what you ought to do.

Flo Kennedy

Men can starve from a lack of self-realization as much as they can from lack of bread.

Richard Wright

If you can't find work that suits you, it may be time for you to take the leap into the entrepreneurship that you always dreamed of.

Chin-Ning Chu

You cannot change the system if you are dependent on it for approval. You have to have the freedom to speak the truth.

Rachel Remen

Freedom can only exist if it is bound to principles and anchored in economics.

Ruby Dee

You have to have a different mind-set. You have to have a mind-set that says [you] can do things.

Eloise Anderson

You cannot make it in this world without a sense of knowing where you are at any given point and what's going on.

Renita Jo Weems

The path to self was paying attention to my intuition, feelings and thoughts. I now include my needs along with what others need or want from me.

Odetta

I want to see more people stepping out of the norm to follow their dreams.

Patricia Russell-McCloud

If there's a book you really want to read but it hasn't been written yet, then you must write it.

Toni Morrison

The man who views the world at 50 the same as he did at 20 has wasted 30 years of his life.

Muhammad Ali

What you are must always displease you, if you would attain to that which you are not.

Saint Augustine

Do you want to control your destiny by creating the career opportunity that matches perfectly with your skills, talents and desires?

Fran Harris

Assume . . . control of your own life, be independent of other people's opinions and make as many important decisions for yourself as possible.

Wayne Dyer

If you are lying on the ground, you must use the ground to raise yourself.

Tibetan proverb

It is a need of the spirit not to forget whoever has let you feel beautiful and safe. But the past is not the next amazing possibility.

June Jordan

Is Your Own Business
What You Want?

I've always seen myself as my own boss. I had a dream, I grabbed it, held it and it manifested itself.

Michele Hoskins

Anyone who needs an alarm clock to wake up is not an entrepreneur.

Jesse L. Jackson

If you want easy, don't become an entrepreneur.

Carol Columbus-Green

Why work for the man? Why not you *be* the man?

Smokey Robinson to Berry Gordy

Being in charge means making decisions, no matter how unpleasant.

Colin Powell

You show me somebody who wants to quit their job and start a business so that they can . . . "not answer to anybody," and I'll show you someone who has no idea of what it means to be an entrepreneur.

Earl G. Graves

When you're the owner of a small business, your business is your boss.

Lorraine Miller

I thought I worked hard with Xerox, but there is no comparison [to the work I do for my own business]. But at the end of the day, I can look back and say, "This is mine."

Paula Inniss

[My mother told me] I could not get ahead working for somebody else.

S. B. Fuller

As more workers continue to fall off the corporate ladder, many displaced executives are discovering only one way to land on their feet: become an entrepreneur.

Heather Page

When I lost my job in 1987, I knew I never
wanted to work for anybody else again.

Claudette Warner-Milne

You're going to find more and more people
returning home to work, especially if your job
is working at the computer.

Jim Shifflett

You don't have to get involved with office politics.
. . . You [can] rely on your own instincts, your
own resources, your own get-up-and-go.

Marlene Connor

If you want to be in business for yourself, you
have to be around people who are in business for
themselves.

John Raye

A career in business is not only a morally serious
vocation but a morally noble one.

Michael Novak

A lot of entrepreneurial businesses were started
not because people wanted to make money but
because they had a larger purpose in mind.

Alfred Marcus

All of my hobbies have turned into business.

Sunny Drewel

I remember someone once said, "The only way to eat an elephant is one bite at a time." This sums up my way of looking at life, but first you have to find your elephant.

Paul Goodnight

I always wanted to discuss the business side of things.

Melvin Van Peebles

We must let people know that the business side [of the music industry] is so rewarding. . . . to have no cutting, no editing. . . . You can just please yourself.

The Artist Formerly Known As Prince

I'm a great believer in owning as much of yourself as possible.

Curtis Mayfield

What I try to do is . . . say to the baseball player: "Have you ever thought about owning your own baseball team?" To the would-be astronaut I ask: "Have you thought about owning the firm that makes the rockets?" There's not enough attention focused on entrepreneurship as a viable career.

Hazel A. King

People start businesses because they think it is
the right thing to do at the right time.

Jere W. Glover

I was tired of making money for other people, so
I went into business for myself.

Lee McCord

There are basically two types of business owners:
the technical expert and the entrepreneur. The
technical expert . . . is considered an expert in
that field. Entrepreneurs, on the other hand . . .
feel their knowledge of the market climate and
general business operation is enough to make
them successful.

Kelvin Boston

In a small company, the standards depend almost
entirely on the entrepreneur's personality, beliefs
and sense of self.

Ronald Berenbeim

For in the end, freedom is a personal and lonely
battle.

Alice Walker

Leadership is a lonely thing, and people who seek
leadership tend to be independent, loner types
who happen to have good social skills.

Richard Hagberg

The thing that makes you exceptional, if you are at all, is inevitably that which must also make you lonely.

Lorraine Hansberry

I'm a sucker for the kids selling candy and magazines on the street . . . because that's where the entrepreneurial skills start.

Leon Jackson

No one has more freedom to refuse to [compromise] than an entrepreneur.

Ronald Berenbeim

The upstart always has to overcome more, just as a start-up business has to struggle with so many more challenges than an established one.

Pat Riley

When you become an entrepreneur, you must be willing to put everything on the line.

Herman Cain

If owning a business is what you want, and you know that's what you want, then begin your planning today.

Kelvin Boston

I can promise you that if you are 100 percent committed to your business it will be difficult for you to fail.

Fran Harris

The smallest firms, those with under five employees, [are] creating the most jobs. We've been following that data from 1989 through 1994 and the trend has continued.

Jere W. Glover

Free enterprise produces an ever-expanding pie.

Andrew Young

It's always better to have your own thing going.

Spike Lee

The most exhilarating, exciting and empowering business experience you can have is being an entrepreneur.

Earl G. Graves

You Need Courage
and Confidence

Today over 15 million Americans—13 percent of
the workforce—are self-employed. Many fantasize
about the possibility of starting their own
business. Few actually do so.

Thomas H. Naylor, William H. Willimon, and Rolf Osterberg

Too many people fear change. They cling to the
familiar old shoe even if it cuts off circulation to
their toes.

Wally "Famous" Amos

Fear keeps us from taking action, and if we don't
act, we never get beyond where we are now.

Jack Canfield

Fear of failure will only limit you, don't be afraid
to take risks.

Barbara Smith

I believe . . . that living on the edge, living in and through your fear, is the summit of life, and that people who refuse to take that dare condemn themselves to a life of living death.

John H. Johnson

One faces down fears of today so that those of tomorrow might be engaged.

Alice Walker

If you are capable, then stop selling yourself short by limiting your imagination.

Chin-Ning Chu

Change has always been led by those whose spirits were bigger than their circumstances.

Jesse L. Jackson

We must change in order to survive.

Pearl Bailey

I'd been making all kinds of money for GE. Maybe I could do the same for myself.

Sandra L. Kurtzig

In the real world you're up against everybody, so you ought to know if you can play or not.

J. Bruce Llewellyn

If you are not courageous enough to take risks you will accomplish nothing in life.

Muhammad Ali

If you take a position that is not popular, you have to be prepared for the kind of criticism that is meted out.

Shirley Chisholm

I had elected, in my fevered search for honorable adjustment to the American scene, not to submit.

Richard Wright

You can do anything you want to do if you want to do it bad enough.

Bill Russell

I have discovered in life that there are ways of getting almost anywhere you want to go, if you really want to go.

Langston Hughes

You make up your mind. You dream the impossible and then do it.

Birdie Hale

When I first started, it was a one-lady operation.
I wore numerous hats, but I have to say I was
never afraid. I enjoyed it.

Flora Green

I'm very sure of myself. . . . I know I'm someone
special. . . . The only limits on me are the ones I
put on myself. I am in control of my thinking.

John Raye

The main thing [for entrepreneurial success] is
you have to be extremely confident. You have to
exude confidence; it has to be dripping out of
your pores.

Rochelle Balch

My grandfather was proud and independent in a
way that only an entrepreneur can be.

Andrew Young

There's no substitute for confidence. You can
have all the talent in the world, but if you don't
believe it, it doesn't mean anything in this
business.

Robert Parish

No one has more confidence in me than I have in
myself.

Allen Iverson

My confidence is in knowing that I have probably trained harder than anyone I am going to run against.

Michael Johnson

You can never get others to believe in you if you don't believe in yourself.

George Fraser

The best way to keep people away from you is not to be good at anything. There's so many people who could be good, could be great, if they tried. . . . Some people are scared to risk it, though.

Charles Barkley

If you trust your nerve as well as your skill, you're capable of a lot more than you can imagine.

Debi Thomas

One thing you want to do to your opponent is make them know they can't win.

Bill Russell

We're very successful. But I think it's very draining to fool yourself into thinking that you'll be able to hobble Microsoft. That's not right. It's not gonna happen.

Bill Gates

Fortune favors the brave.

Terence

I don't think I was courageous. I think I was determined.

Daisy Bates

I thank Mike [Tyson] for the opportunity. It was a challenge. A lot of kids are scared of challenges. But if you believe in yourself . . . you can do anything. It takes work, it takes prayer.

Evander Holyfield

I *am* the toughest golfer mentally.

Tiger Woods

The gods help them that help themselves.

Aesop

Initiative

Young people are recognizing that they've got to be more responsible for their own destiny. For many of them that means starting their own company.

Bill Bygrave

If you do something it's OK. But if you're lazy you will not be happy.

Daisy Gonwe

You have to ask, "What can I do for myself?" Then go out and do it.

J. Bruce Llewellyn

You first have to do a thing one time before you know what you can do.

Osceola McCarty

Man often becomes what he believes himself to be. . . . If I have the belief that I can do it, I shall surely acquire the capacity to do it even if I may not have it in the beginning.

Mahatma Gandhi

Each and every one of us has to demonstrate individual initiative to close the gap between what our community has and what it needs.

Ed Lewis

Find a need and fill it. . . . Study the people around [you]. How do they live? What makes them tick? What do they want? Out of these questions, out of a real need, came the first substantial Gaston business.

A. G. Gaston

Leadership is not about knowledge, about being the smartest. It's about results.

Jack Zenger

When my father lost his job, I thought the family was going to starve, but he created an opportunity out of a very dismal situation. He started his own business.

Terrie Williams

I didn't like the options in the job market, so I started my own business.

Alvin Foster

I was tired of training my managers to become my boss.

Karen I. Duckett

I realized that I was going to keep getting fired if I lived up to my own principles; therefore, the only way not to get fired again was to start my own company.

Barbara Proctor

[When my job was eliminated] I started my own enterprise . . . which . . . guarantees me ownership of my voice and opinions.

Barbara Reynolds

I felt I was ready to make my own business decisions and to accept responsibility for the associated risks that came with it.

Pauline C. Brooks

I wanted to control my own destiny and [I was willing] to take risks.

Don Barden

Living off music seemed better than living off the land.

B. B. King

If I had to single out one element in my life that has made a difference for me, it would be a passion to compete.

Sam Walton

Each of us must take the initiative to create our opportunities, not waiting around for favors. We must not assume a door is closed but must push on it.

Marian Wright Edelman

People ought to listen to their hearts. The voice of truth is there all the time, telling us where to go, how to do it.

Denyce Graves

The life of wisdom must be a life of contemplation combined with action.

M. Scott Peck

Whatever your plans and goals, you must honestly look into yourself and know that you will give all that it takes to reach your objectives. You don't get anything in life without taking a chance.

Terrie Williams

Don't wait for somebody to give you a chance; take a chance.

Janet Cheatham Bell

I don't know what's going to happen, but I didn't want to sit at home and do "shoulda-coulda-woulda."

Jackie Joyner-Kersee

Whatever you can do to slap the cold water of joy into your face every morning, you've got to do that.

Bobby McFerrin

You have to expect things of yourself before you can do them.

Michael Jordan

Belief
Initiates and guides action—
Or it does nothing.

Octavia Butler

The entrepreneur seeks new challenges, excitement, unpredictable results, and adventure; in this sense, he would make a poor bureaucrat.

David C. McClelland

Business owners with less than 20 employees [have] created 6.3 million jobs.

Rieva Lesonsky

Entrepreneurship [is] the ultimate smart money move.

Kelvin Boston

And Opportunity

I had always wanted to become an entrepreneur, and [McDonald's Business Development Program] was my chance.

Ronald E. Damper

I realized that every corporate building I stepped into had fresh flowers and plants on display. I knew there was a market.

Saundra Parks

When I serviced the stores in my territory, I noticed that the items with the fastest turnover were the snack foods.

James A. Lindsay

Everything is timing. In the fashion business, when things start erupting, you need to be there.

John Bernard

I basically felt that given my experience in the toy business . . . if I didn't [create multicultural toys], I didn't know who would.

Jacob R. Miles

When my modeling career was over, it seemed natural to open a restaurant that would offer the different kinds of food I loved and that would provide a gathering place for the rich variety of people I enjoyed meeting.

Barbara Smith

I'm a man . . . just following my dreams and taking advantage of opportunities that come my way.

Shaquille O'Neal

This is a tremendous time to be your own boss. The opportunities are out there for the taking.

Cheryl D. Broussard

Some . . . turn away from competition and pull back in the face of opportunity. Some even mess up their lives deliberately in order to force themselves out of the game.

Clarence Page

When you realize that you can be your own best friend or your own worst enemy, then you stop blaming others and start to get out of the way of your own progress.

Louis Farrakhan

I had to make my own living and my own opportunity. . . . Don't sit down and wait for the opportunities to come; you have to get up and make them.

Madame C. J. Walker

It is at the bottom of life we must begin, and not at the top. Nor should we permit our grievances to overshadow our opportunities.

Booker T. Washington

You can't invent events. They just happen. But you have to be prepared to deal with them when they happen.

Constance Baker Motley

There is no future in a lack of vision.

Robert Miller

When you are looking for obstacles, you can't find opportunities.

Janet Cheatham Bell

At the root of every challenge, I see an opportunity.

Earl G. Graves

It's better to be prepared for an opportunity and not have one than to have an opportunity and not be prepared.

Whitney Young

The ones that have the opportunity ought to take advantage of it and to help those who don't have it.

John Hope Franklin

He who does not improve himself by the motives and opportunities afforded by this world gives the best evidence that he would not improve in any other world.

Frederick Douglass

The purest negotiations occur when you have plenty of other prospects in the pipeline and plenty of money in the bank.

Danielle Kennedy

I've always felt that if we try hard enough, we can do a lot of things. The opportunities in this country are unlimited.

James M. Woods, Sr.

There is no shortage of opportunity. If you say yes to something, whether it turns out to be good or bad, you still have to say no to the next thing that comes along because you have already filled that space.

Joanna Tamer

The offer of opportunity in a free society carries with it the requirement of hard work.

Doug Wilder

The doors of opportunity are always closed. You have to put your foot on the door and kick it down.

Pervis Spann

In this country about 16 percent of our businesses are new every year, and when that rate declines, the economy goes into recession.

Bruce D. Phillips

[The Digital Economy] is an environment that favors small, agile businesses that can respond quickly to the marketplace.

Don Tapscott

The opportunities for younger people are now more [plentiful] than ever before. These people can start their own businesses and graduate [from college] as the president of a company.

Jennifer Kushell

You Must Be Creative

Every business needs to be looking for creativity in everything it does.

Kathleen R. Allen

The emerging movements toward economic self-reliance will not be led by political action but by creative entrepreneurship.

Ron Watkins

Now business seeks a new advantage—delicate and dangerous, and absolutely vital—the creativity advantage.

John Kao

One of the keys to making a business succeed is to link it with other businesses and with customers in creative ways.

James Moore

Today creativity always ends up as
entertainment, not as what it originally was:
sustenance of the spirit and of the mind.

Toni Morrison

Regardless of the circumstances, you can use your
mind and creative talent to do what you want.

Jimmy McJamerson

I never predetermine my game. It's always creative.

Michael Jordan

When you're creating your own shit . . . even the
sky ain't the limit.

Miles Davis

True wisdom consists not only in seeing what
is before your eyes, but in foreseeing what is to
come.

Terence

Don't let preconceived ideas dictate how you plot
your course. Be open to nontraditional ways of
doing things.

Clark Childers

Criticism doesn't stifle ideas—it makes them
better.

Jack Ricchiuto

One head does not exchange ideas.

Ashanti proverb

You can't use up creativity. The more you use, the more you have. Sadly, too often creativity is smothered rather than nurtured.

Maya Angelou

Your creative ability is developed by competition because when you compete, you have to outthink the opposition.

Edward G. Gardner

If you're prepared to improvise . . . you can enjoy being creative all the more.

Barbara Smith

You become a winner by maintaining an innovation trajectory that is critically important to other members of the community. . . . The lesson for all businesses is the need to innovate and to keep innovating.

James Moore

Conformity to the status quo is a real enemy of creativity.

Mike Vance

The world has improved mostly through people who are unorthodox, who do unorthodox things.

Ruby Dee

I wanted to have my own record company. . . . I wanted to have creative control.

Bobbi Humphrey

In the Digital Economy, the main assets are contained in the heads of the people who work for the company . . . because innovation is what's driving this economy.

Don Tapscott

You want to build your industry, but you don't want to lose market share at the same time. The only way to [prevent this] is to innovate.

Robert Imbriale

Creativity is a business survival skill.

Roger von Oech

Creativity is the sudden cessation of stupidity.

Edwin H. Land

My experience is that owners of privately held businesses are much less fearful of creativity.

Lou Pritchett

Since new developments are the products of
a creative mind, we must therefore stimulate
and encourage that type of mind in every way
possible.

George Washington Carver

The real beginning point for creativity is
emptying your mind—pushing out the ideas
you know to be true.

Raymond Gleason

Anything we do that forces us out of our normal
environment will let us see things in new, different
ways.

Kathleen R. Allen

The truth about business innovations [is] that
most of them don't involve a flash, just a
flashlight. It's a search party.

Dale Dauten

Of course we want breakthrough, audacious
ideas. But we also need small, incremental ideas
for making things better.

Jack Zenger

Much creativity lies in what seems like small
ideas.

Roger von Oech

When you're overwhelmed with the day-to-day details of running your business, it's hard to distance yourself enough to come up with [new ideas, so you need time away].

Joanne Brooks

Creativity can be developed in all of us. . . . Practice is why the truly creative stay truly creative—and it's how all of us can get much more creative.

Jack Ricchiuto

Never underestimate the creative pleasure that drives many who find their calling in business.

Michael Novak

Think and Plan Carefully

The mind is the standard of the man.

Paul Laurence Dunbar

[My father] taught me that the most powerful weapon you have is your mind.

Andrew Young

The greatest imprisonment of all, and therefore, the greatest freedom, too, is in your mind.

Patrice Gaines

It is your mental attitude which creates results in your life.

Wally "Famous" Amos

In today's new economy . . . the minds of gifted people are what truly distinguish one organization from another.

John Kao

The bottom line is to ensure survival, and the best way to do that is to use your head.

Anne Ashmore

You can accomplish a lot with nothing but physical gifts and intuitive reflex. But the mind is the only place that can comprehend the truly great, and it's the best weapon any of us has when it comes time to perform.

Michael Johnson

He who upsets a thing should know how to rearrange it.

Sierra Leone proverb

We can endure almost anything if we are centered, if we have some focus in our life. You can endure if you have an anchor.

Renita Jo Weems

In every occupation, focus is vital.

Mary Kay Ash

Focus on what you want to accomplish and you can do it.

Lupe Anguiano

Hurry, hurry has no blessing.

Swahili proverb

We really have to learn to love thinking again.
Not fretting, not worrying, but thinking. . . .
Thinking and learning are what we are born for.

Toni Morrison

That which you think about expands. Therefore,
develop the habit of always focusing on what you
want, not on what you don't want.

Wayne Dyer

A man is what he thinks about all day long.

Ralph Waldo Emerson

Human thought, like God, makes the world in its
own image.

Adam Clayton Powell, Jr.

All your scholarship . . . would be in vain, if at
the same time you do not build your character
and attain mastery over your thoughts and
actions.

Mahatma Gandhi

Thoughts are energy and you can make your world or break your world by your thinking.

Susan L. Taylor

If you think good thoughts, you're going to live good thoughts.

John Lewis

Age may wrinkle the face, but lack of enthusiasm wrinkles the soul.

Wally "Famous" Amos

There is nothing so easy but that it becomes difficult when you do it reluctantly.

Terence

A wise person decides slowly but abides by these decisions.

Arthur Ashe

Our plan is to lead the public with new products rather than ask them what kind of products they want. The public does not know what is possible, but we do.

Akio Morita

Spend time planning and the project will go smoothly; good plans make a job easier and cheaper to implement.

Alvin Foster

Everything could be planned, but nothing [is] ever promised.

Patti LaBelle

Don't count your chickens before they hatch.

Aesop

The know-how and ingenuity of the people who use computers . . . can be linked together to create a higher order of thinking and knowledge.

Don Tapscott

We shall
    think—
    plan—
See the day whole through our assaulted
  vision.

Gwendolyn Brooks in "Song of Winnie"

Set Your Goals

The tragedy in life doesn't lie in not reaching your goal. The tragedy lies in having no goal to reach.

Benjamin E. Mays

Figure out what you want out of life, then set your goals and maintain them as long as it is biologically possible.

Clint Eastwood

In order to plan effective goals, you must set them in stages.

Cheryl D. Broussard

The difference between a goal and a wish is: a wish you never do anything about; a goal, you *do* something about.

John Raye

Miniaturization and compactness have always appealed to the Japanese. And we set as our goal a radio small enough to fit into a shirt pocket.

Akio Morita

Making and keeping promises to ourselves precedes making and keeping promises to others.

Stephen R. Covey

To do our best work, we feel we have to have *control*.

Terry Lewis

Goal-setting is the master skill. . . . It is through the practice of goal-setting that one can compensate for life's shortcomings, whether those shortcomings be real—lack of money, limited schooling, or poor self-image—or imagined.

Dennis Kimbro and Napoleon Hill

If something is important, do it immediately, even if it's a sacrifice.

Milton Gralla

It is never too late—and you never have too little money—to establish financial goals and put a plan into motion to achieve them.

Audrey Edwards

Set your goals. Make the commitments and stick with them until they become a reality.

Sandra Williams Bate

My strength [is] staying focused, visualizing what the next step is, making sure of the adventure and doing it.

Dennis Rodman

The ship's captain cannot see his destination for fully 99 percent of his journey—but he knows what it is, where it is, and that he will reach it if he keeps doing certain things a certain way.

Dennis Kimbro and Napoleon Hill

I have no hobbies and play no games, and the food and drink of my life is trying to succeed.

John H. Johnson

I've always known where I wanted to go in life. I've never let anything deter me. This is my purpose. It will unfold.

Tiger Woods

Acting is just a way of making a living, the family is life.

Denzel Washington

I've done well keeping the business small, and I've never been the kind of entrepreneur who thinks she has to make a million dollars to be successful.

Claudette Warner-Milne

I'm in business for more than one thing. I do sell art to people who buy art; I want people to be able to talk about it. Art to me is like a passion.

June Kelly

It took from the time I was 17 . . . 'til I was 45 to make the decision that [art] was what I really wanted to do. I couldn't live the rest of my life without doing it.

Ed Dwight

How can a man live out the length of his days without a vision-prize?

Leon Forrest

I never had a plan in my life. I had goals and objectives, but not a plan. . . . If you do a good job, the next step will unfold itself to you.

J. Bruce Llewellyn

If you reach for what you want, what you want will be put within your reach.

Janet Cheatham Bell

Hear All Kinds of Advice

There will always be those who are ready to speak persuasively about the utter impossibilities of your achievement, or the minuscule chances of your success as you venture forth. Consider their words, if you must, then proceed to go your own way. Listen instead to the inner rhythms of the music within your soul.

Dennis Kimbro and Napoleon Hill

There are as many opinions as there are men.

Terence

A word to the wise ain't necessary; it's the stupid ones who need advice.

Bill Cosby

Only our actions are noted, not what we have read or what we have spoken.

Mahatma Gandhi

When you hear a man talking, always inquire as to what he has done. . . . Oratory and resolutions do not avail much.

Carter G. Woodson

We have too many high sounding words, and too few actions that correspond with them.

Abigail Adams

Beware the naked man who offers you his shirt.

Harvey Mackay

If you keep going to a dry well, you will never quench your thirst.

B. Denise Owens

Only when you have crossed the river can you say the crocodile has a lump on his snout.

Ashanti proverb

I sought advice and cooperation from all those around, but not permission.

Muhammad Ali

Never trust the advice of a man in difficulties.

Aesop

Some people will tear you down just to see you fall. They'll do it even if your loss is their own.

Walter Mosley

Never be limited by other people's limited imaginations. . . . If you adopt their attitudes, then the possibility won't exist because you'll have already shut it out. . . . You can hear other people's wisdom, but you've got to re-evaluate the world for yourself.

Mae Jemison

This old notion of swallowing down other peoples' ideas and problems just as they have worked them out without putting [your] brain and originality into it and making them applicable to [your] specific needs must go.

George Washington Carver

Learn All You Can

Would-be entrepreneurs have to be informed consumers. You can save big bucks . . . if you spend just a small amount of time educating yourself.

Elizabeth King

In the business world I always strove to learn as much as I could.

Jackie Robinson

Knowledge can be obtained [even] under difficulties.

Frederick Douglass

There are two kinds of knowledge. One is general, the other is specialized. General knowledge . . . is of but little use in the accumulation of money.

Napoleon Hill

Learn a business. Nothing is going to help if you don't have the basic fundamentals for your business.

Bob Johnson

In a lot of ways, entrepreneurship is the interdisciplinary business major of the 21st century.

Allan Bailey

This [Internet] is a whole new medium of human communication, and you need to know about it because it is changing all the rules of how we do business.

Don Tapscott

It is the fool whose own tomatoes are sold to him.

Akan proverb

Not to know is bad; not to wish to know is worse.

Nigerian proverb

If you can't count, they can cheat you. If you can't read, they can beat you.

Toni Morrison

In a knowledge-based economy, work and learning become the same thing. . . . Added value is created primarily by brains, not brawn.

Don Tapscott

The more research you do, the more credible you are. And the bigger the sale, the more essential research is.

Brian Tracy

Young people should never accept a limit on their horizons. In fact, older people shouldn't either. Learn everything there is to know.

Gordon Parks

I wanted to see what was going on in all of music. Knowledge is freedom and ignorance is slavery, and I just couldn't . . . be that close to freedom and not take advantage of it.

Miles Davis

I had such a thirsty mind, I wanted to learn everything.

Quincy Jones

One's work may be finished some day, but one's education never.

Alexandre Dumas, *pere*

I suddenly appreciated what real education might be. I vowed, right then, to learn something new every day. . . . At that moment my life was changed.

Amiri Baraka

I talk about education. It is the key to our salvation. Knowledge is power.

Johnnie Cochran

A free curiosity has more efficacy in learning than a frightful enforcement.

Saint Augustine

There's no need to overpower when you can outsmart.

Phil Jackson

I want them to be educated enough to know when someone is trying to take advantage of them. We're creating producers, not consumers.

Catherine Schaller

Filmmaking is a craft and it can be learned like anything else.

Spike Lee

There's no magic potion or hocus-pocus [to successful teaching]. It's simply believing everyone can learn if they put forth the effort.

Abdulalim Shabazz

Wisdom is not like money to be tied up and hidden.

Akan proverb

Everyone doing his best is not the answer. It is first necessary that people know what to do.

W. Edwards Deming

Knowledge is the key that unlocks all the doors. It doesn't matter what you look like or where you come from if you have knowledge.

Benjamin S. Carson, Sr.

I continue to learn invaluable lessons about how to lead by observing the greats who came before me.

Andre Harrell

Know what you can do and go ahead and do it.

John Lewis

The minute you can develop yourself so you excel in whatever you do, then you are going to find that you don't have any real problems.

S. B. Fuller

Education remains the key to both economic and political empowerment.

Barbara Jordan

People who think education is expensive have never counted the cost of ignorance.

Andrew Young

Knowledge is only *potential* power. It becomes power only when, and if, it is organized into a definite plan of action and directed to a definite end.

Napoleon Hill

They built a schoolhouse
        . . . and
they sat around it
            With guns
for it was a jewel
casting brilliances into the future

Mari Evans in "The Schoolhouse"

There Will Be Obstacles

No matter how much upside or downside
planning you do, there'll always be something
to come along and blindside you.

Sandra L. Kurtzig

Obstacles come from every direction and
you have to keep solid footing and know that
whatever comes your way, you'll handle it. God
will show you how.

Terrie Williams

In all endeavors, there are obstacles to confront.
One of the secrets of success is to refuse to allow
temporary setbacks to defeat us.

Mary Kay Ash

When you have a big enough dream in your
heart, you can overcome almost any obstacle.

Les Brown

If my life stands for anything, it's that you can make it in this country, despite all the obstacles.

Johnnie Cochran

You have to be prepared to lose before you can win.

Marjorie Margolies-Mezvinsky

Every time I fail, I know I'm that much closer to the success I want.

Wayne Allyn Root

All progress is precarious, and the solution of one problem brings us face to face with another problem.

Martin Luther King, Jr.

I'm self-employed and have the same problems that small-business people have—cash flow and daily operations—but I run a very viable business.

Faith Childs

Any problem can be solved using the materials in the room.

Edwin H. Land

The way we see the problem *is* the problem.

Stephen R. Covey

Problems come from a lack of knowledge, not a lack of trying.

David Guidry

A problem is a chance for you to do your best.

Duke Ellington

The difference between businesses that succeed and those that fail is the ability of the entrepreneur to lead the company through countless problems that growth will bring.

Bryan Drysdale and Julie Blau

That's why a lot of businesses have fallen by the wayside—you have one entrepreneur or family that owns a business and keeps it close to the vest, but in terms of . . . setting up a structure for long-term growth and preservation of your company, it's a little shortsighted.

Derrick Dingle

When I started out I was doing about 90 percent Creative and 10 percent Business. . . . [I was] now doing about 98 percent Business and 2 percent Creative. I was stuck and I hated it.

Berry Gordy

It is in this whole process of meeting and solving problems that life has its meaning. Problems are the cutting edge that distinguishes between success and failure. . . . Wise people learn not to dread, but actually to welcome problems.

M. Scott Peck

Not every moment is one of energy, light and happiness.

Jessye Norman

In knowing how to overcome little things, a centimeter at a time, gradually when bigger things come, you're prepared.

Katherine Dunham

In all of life, there are sequential states of growth and development.

Stephen R. Covey

Your business will not grow if you arrange your actions around the attempt to avoid all problems.

Bryan Drysdale and Julie Blau

We must accept finite disappointment, but we must never lose infinite hope.

Martin Luther King, Jr.

Difficulties exist to be surmounted.

Ralph Waldo Emerson

Continuous challenges always inspire me.

Edward G. Gardner

Every experience has a lesson. . . . You give
things power over yourself, and then they own
you.

Wally "Famous" Amos

There is no problem of human nature which is
insoluble.

Ralph J. Bunche

Every crisis has both its dangers and
opportunities. It can spell either salvation
or doom.

Martin Luther King, Jr.

In your moments of challenge, you will need a
vision of how . . . to go above and beyond.

Pat Riley

I believed there was nothing I couldn't conquer.
God never put an obstacle in my way that I
couldn't get around.

Rae Lewis-Thornton

If you want to win big, you will lose big along the way.

Wayne Allyn Root

Nothing on earth can stand in the way of a well-thought-out plan backed by persistence and determination.

Dennis Kimbro and Napoleon Hill

If You're Black

For every 1,000 Arabs in America, there are 108 business starts; for Asians, it's 96 and whites, 64. For every 1,000 African Americans, there are only nine business starts.

Joe Davidson

The first 244 years of the black experience in America was one of slavery—forced labor without income, wealth producing without wealth accumulation.

Audrey Edwards and Craig K. Polite

For the want of business habits and training, our energies have become paralyzed.

Martin Delany

Here in this country, there is a certain conspiratorial desire—regardless of what you do, how much you earn, you're still black. And that's meant to demean. But it only demeans you if you allow it to.

Reginald F. Lewis

Discrimination is terrible, but you've got to live. . . . You can't waste psychological energy on feeling downtrodden.

Anne Wortham

Economic and demographic change can be made to work for, not against, African American entrepreneurs.

Julianne Malveaux

Instead of saying, "Hey, let us in," we need to create the same empire. We have the money, the talent. It's whether or not we have the will to do so.

Bill Stephney

Money is America's god and business people can dig black power if it coincides with green power.

Jackie Robinson

Blacks . . . don't realize it doesn't kill your soul to be a capitalist.

Bundy Gambrell

Welfare reform is coming and we can't depend on other people to give us jobs. If we want to make it in this world, we have to be self-empowered.

Sy Bounds

The poor people in my Manhattan neighborhood long ago discovered workfare. . . . The freelance recycling business has become the leading street industry.

Michael Lewis

Those guys [who financed *Get on the Bus*] have done a great inspirational thing by taking over the financing. Now it is time [for African Americans to take] step two, which is the marketing.

Warrington Hudlin

Spike [Lee] is a marketing wizard. He really has a way of capitalizing on every opportunity, which is good. We don't need another starving artist martyr to add to the junk pile of undercapitalized African American filmmakers.

Ken Smikle

[The group of black entrepreneurs and financial experts talked] of wooing white corporations into business partnerships [instead] of boycotting them. They called for improving the quality of black businesses, rather than expecting them to thrive on blind racial loyalty.

Byron P. White

We [must] not see ourselves as victims. . . . and we have . . . to move from being the victim of other people's decisions to the architect of our own well-being.

Lani Guinier

In my career, I found the most important thing is not to be self-conscious about [race] and not to let it interfere with the way you think or the manner in which you operate.

Reginald F. Lewis

If I'm the head of the black division of a large company I can't pass that job on to my son. But I can pass the company that I own on to him.

Bill Stephney

The black community would be healthier if successful business people were treated like heroes and made into role models.

Dorothy Brunson

Starting a business can provide some young people with a greatly needed alternative to dealing drugs while helping to increase their self-esteem.

Melissa Bradley

Kids need to see that there are parts of life other than sports that they can aspire to and still be successful.

Bob Wilburn

Black parents are still telling their children to get a good education to get a good job, not to start their own business.

Jawanza Kunjufu

When you work with high risk youth, make them entrepreneurs because then they will be too busy making money to do other [negative] things.

Ronald Johnson

I believe that if black people have their souls right and their pockets full, then they are free.

Buster Soaries

There are certain people that aren't used to being told what to do by a 6'4," 220 pound black man who is a director. I'm supposed to be either robbing their car or opening their door.

Bill Duke

The stories told about me by others, I could not accept because I lacked dignity [in them]. . . . And I knew I had [dignity], so it was necessary for me to tell my own story.

Chinua Achebe

The question, the only question, was what were we going to do with what we had in order to make things better for ourselves.

John H. Johnson

If anybody's going to help African American people, it's got to be ourselves.

Magic Johnson

Our current economic condition as a people does not have to be the indicator of our economic future.

Audrey Edwards

To make a difference . . . you need to do big catalytic developments. . . . So if we make a difference on the worst blocks in the neighborhood and turn around the climate, private investors can come in behind us.

Susan McCann

No one else can retrieve our values and salvage our people better than we can.

Dorothy I. Height

Through the centuries of despair and dislocation, we had been creative, because we faced down death by daring to hope.

Maya Angelou

We are a people with passion and creativity in abundance.

George Fraser

If you live in an oppressive society, you've got to be very resilient. You can't let each little thing crush you. You have to take every encounter and make yourself larger, rather than allow yourself to be diminished by it.

James Earl Jones

It is time for blacks to begin the shift from a wartime to a peacetime identity, from fighting for opportunity to the seizing of it.

Shelby Steele

No one owns the black consumer market. What you should ask is who can capitalize on the market, and that is those individuals who are primed and geared to grasp opportunity.

Dennis Kimbro

It's important to get more African Americans in [the apparel] industry because I see the money that's made. I know how much money we spend on clothing, and it bothers me that we are not reaping some of those benefits.

Clotee McAfee

As the South Side [of Chicago] has deteriorated, it has made the bootlegger [taxi] stronger. No meter operation will come out here. We had to create something because we weren't getting the service.

James Palmer

It's always been my belief that all the ingredients are in place to create a black film studio and black film industry. The audience is there, the talent is there and the money is there. What has been missing is the catalyst—a focal point—to bring it together.

Robert L. Johnson

This is the golden age of opportunity for persons of color in the U.S. We are shaking off the dry bones of ignorance, jealousy and envy. We are witnessing the beginning of a movement of unity among black people and this time it can't be stopped.

John Raye

We must want to do more than merely survive, we must want to succeed. Our greatest challenge is to remember who we are—the people who refused to die—and to do the work. This is the appointed hour. We can choose. We can change.

Susan L. Taylor

All you golden-black children of the sun,
Lift up! and read the sky
Written in the tongue of your ancestors.
It is yours, claim it.

Henry L. Dumas, in "Black Star Line"

If You're a Woman

When you trade a man for *the man*, you still got somebody telling you how to live your life.

Johnnie Tillmon-Blackston

My primary motivation for going into business was to help women.

Mary Kay Ash

It's important for women business owners to be themselves. . . . I was a wife, mother and a professional and I managed a household. I bring all of that into my capacity as a CEO.

Loida Nicolas Lewis

I think bonding between women business owners is essential. The sharing of information will be vital to our survival.

Terrie Williams

Being taken seriously is still one of the biggest challenges women entrepreneurs face.

Sharon Hadary

Because I am a woman, [the 30 percent annual growth rate] of my company is seen as a fluke.

Dorothy Brunson

A major challenge for women continues to be access to capital.

Emma Chappell

People are just not very ambitious for women, still. Your son you want to be the best he can be. Your daughter you want to be happy.

Alexa Canady

The future woman must have a life work and economic independence.

W. E. B. DuBois

We as women must develop and integrate our full range of skills.

Beverley Anderson-Manley

Both black and white women tend to open businesses in the services and retail fields, which require greater time involvement of the owners and generate smaller receipts.

Lois Harry

I'm moving away from being a lonely designer working in her studio to being a businesswoman.

Courtney Sloane

When you are female and black and you start talking about doing mergers, you are not taken seriously.

Dorothy Brunson

Most financial institutions have been and continue to be reluctant to make loans to black women. . . . Officers of these institutions have difficulty accepting [black women] as authentic, competent business persons.

Lois Harry

Given the obstacles that exist for every black woman in America, sisters so visible at the top of the American power ladder must be exceptional.

Patricia Reid-Merritt

Black women do experience a glass ceiling, but
first they hit a concrete wall.

Ella L. J. Edmondson Bell

You could say race was an obstacle to me, you
could say sex was an obstacle to me, but I refused
to own them in that way.

Eleanor Holmes Norton

There are [many] areas where black women can
excel, but they have to have some foundation
from which to transfer their skills from employee
to entrepreneur.

Dorothy Brunson

I buried Superwoman. And in doing so I found
my strengths.

Rae Lewis-Thornton

African American girls have to think beyond jobs.
We really need to think about owning our own
organizations, building our own companies. That's
the only way that we'll ever be really empowered.

Susan L. Taylor

The timidity and retiring disposition of women
unfit them for the strife, competition and worry
of business life. But we must do something . . .
because our needs . . . and our ambitions force
us to enter the world and contend for a living.

Maggie Lena Walker

In this [entertainment] business, an African American woman has to protect herself because precious few [others] will. . . . I won't put my life in the hands of fate or in the hands of anyone who doesn't know me.

Anita Baker

The Bobbi Humphrey School of Business is not about getting mad—it's about getting *paid*.

Bobbi Humphrey

If a man mulls over a decision, they say, "He's weighing the options." If a woman does it, they say, "She can't make up her mind."

Barbara Proctor

They say I'm a witch with a "b" on the front. It's the age-old problem. Someone else would be called a shrewd businessman. Women are called other things.

Anita Baker

Women have particular difficulties starting and maintaining businesses. Not only must they travel the rough road to start-up, but at times battle sexism at the hands of black men who leave women out of their success networks.

Ernest Holsendolph

The nature of what I do is very challenging. I eliminate anything that is considered an obstacle. I never say, "Because I'm female, or black, or over 30, there's a problem." . . . I never make it a problem for me, so why should it be a problem for you?

C. C. H. Pounder

As black women continue to grow their businesses and turn profits, the old boy network will stand up and take notice.

Barbara Landers Bowles

That [black women] have "made it" as independent business owners provides evidence that it is indeed possible . . . to attain success on their own terms.

Lois Harry

I am a product of every other black woman before me who has done or said anything worthwhile. Recognizing that I am a part of that history is what allows me to soar.

Oprah Winfrey

Women are the ones who can bring about profound changes. We've asked men to change, but they created these structures and they believe in them. What they want is to maintain the status quo.

Bella Abzug

Fifty percent of all U.S. jobs created in the last three years were created by entrepreneurial women.

Janean Chun

Women hold 626 of a total 6,123 Fortune 500 board seats.

Catalyst

Those boards without women are missing out on valuable input.

John H. Bryan

We cannot allow an obstacle—racism, sexism, ageism, classism, sexual harassment, whatever it is—to hold us back.

Terrie Williams

As a woman, you know up front that you're not on an equal playing field—that you will have to fight harder and be more patient than men—and so you acknowledge it and move on.

Faye Dunaway

Women are changing the face of success, not from masculine to feminine but by proving success doesn't come in one shape, size or color.

Patty DeDominic

In two generations, we've gone from women not having checkbooks to passing the Equal Opportunity Credit Act to all these women starting businesses.

Emily Card

Women indeed know their place. It's at the helm of their very own companies.

Janean Chun

And You'll Make Mistakes

So many entrepreneurs feel personally responsible for every job [and] have difficulty passing on authority to employees.

David Newton

You're not always going to be successful, but if you're scared to fail, you don't deserve to be successful.

Charles Barkley

Never be consumed by today's problems. In time they will work out. Always live each day as it comes.

Gloria Knight

Every problem does not need to be solved.

Michael Owens

Too many people overvalue what they're not and undervalue what they are.

Malcolm Forbes

Imperfections make us perfect. The things we might not like, or that make us different from other people, are what make us very unique.

Iman

Failure is the really bad "F-word." . . . It's something you can't be afraid of, because you'll stop growing. . . . The next step beyond failure could be your biggest success in life.

Debbie Allen

Losing is as integral a part of the dance [of life] as winning. . . . Only by acknowledging the possibility of defeat can you fully experience the joy of competition.

Phil Jackson

I don't know the key to success, but the key to failure is trying to please everybody.

Bill Cosby

Ninety-nine percent of the failures come from people who have the habit of making excuses.

George Washington Carver

He makes his failure certain by himself being the first person convinced of it.

Alexandre Dumas, *fils*

The lack of expectation of success takes away a powerful incentive to succeed.

George Subira

I feel the most important requirement in success is learning to overcome failure. You must learn to tolerate it, but never accept it.

Reggie Jackson

You never fail until you stop trying.

Florence Griffith-Joyner

It's not failure if you enjoyed the process.

Oprah Winfrey

Don't be afraid of failing. It's the way you learn to do things right.

Marian Wright Edelman

If you do fail, don't be afraid to draw on it for inspiration. . . . Failure deepens us . . . gives us great wisdom.

Michael Johnson

Not everyone can win all the time; obsessing
about winning adds an unnecessary layer of
pressure that constricts body and spirit and,
ultimately, robs you of the freedom to do your best.

Phil Jackson

Millions of people . . . don't see that by spending
their lives afraid of failure, their lives *become*
failures.

Wayne Allyn Root

If you look at a situation that is disastrous if you
do nothing, then you have to do something.

Benjamin S. Carson, Sr.

All you have left after a crisis is your conduct
during it.

Johnnie Cochran

Mistakes are a fact of life. It is the response to
the error that counts.

Nikki Giovanni

Life [is] a series of lessons and you have to study
your mistakes to succeed.

Patrice Gaines

Mistakes are part of the fun.

Barbara Smith

It's important that you face life as it is, not as you wish it could be.

Brian Tracy

Experience is not what happens to a man; it's what a man does with what happens to him.

Aldous Huxley

But You Can Start Over

Instead of waiting for things to get better, make a list of all the things you can do until your situation improves.

Danielle Kennedy

Those who take action and find creative solutions to their disappointments and challenges are thrivers. Their reward is the life of their dreams.

Wayne Allyn Root

You may feel awful when something doesn't work out—but later, you'll be amazed how happy you are that it didn't. If it had worked out, the new opportunity that is in front of you now never would have presented itself.

Joanna Tamer

If you try to live off the past, you can get stung in the present.

Michael Jordan

If a choice turns out to be something I regret, I let it go. I try not to blame myself, because you can't call things back, and if you do, it comes with a price.

Ruby Dee

I have no excuses. We all lose in life. It's how you come back from losing that matters.

Mike Tyson

Defeat should not be the source of discouragement, but a stimulus to keep plotting.

Shirley Chisholm

When life knocks you down, try to fall on your back because if you can look up, you can get up.

Les Brown

It doesn't matter how many times you fall down. What matters is how many times you get up.

Marian Wright Edelman

Do not look where you fell, but where you slipped.

African proverb

I must use the manure that has been thrown on me to fertilize myself and grow from seed again.

Eartha Kitt

[Slaying the Dragon] is a book about how to . . . keep going after you lose the biggest race of your life. . . . You will. I did several times.

Michael Johnson

Our greatest glory is not in never failing, but in rising every time we fall.

Confucius

Each small victory improves the odds that you will triumph at the moment of truth.

Pat Riley

The commonsense approach is to build from your own base and assimilate instead of being assimilated.

John H. Johnson

Put that smile on your face and keep living.

Magic Johnson

A bitter person is a person in the process of destroying himself. I wasn't going to destroy myself. I was going to make something out of my life.

Dempsey Travis

My philosophy is that not only are you responsible for your life, but doing the best at this moment puts you in the best place for the next moment.

Oprah Winfrey

My stepfather . . . taught me that sometimes what appears to be a complicated problem can have a simple solution.

Reginald F. Lewis

Anybody who is in a position to discipline others should first learn to accept discipline himself.

Malcolm X

Everything I need to get over in this world is inside . . . connecting me to everybody and everything that's ever been. . . . I can't live inside yesterday's pain, but I can't live without it.

George C. Wolfe

Fate is the raw materials of experience. They come uninvited and often unanticipated. Destiny is what a man does with these raw materials.

Howard Thurman

No man was ever so completely skilled in the conduct of life as not to receive new information from age and experience.

Terence

I'm having a good time now because this is what I want to do. Now that's power—owning your own life.

Linda Shepard

My future starts when I wake up every morning. . . . wake up and see the first light. Then, I'm grateful, and I can't wait to wake up, because there's something new to do and try every day.

Miles Davis

God gave me strength
And it don't make sense
Not to keep on pushing

Curtis Mayfield

Without faith, nothing is possible. With it, nothing is impossible.

Mary McLeod Bethune

There is no shortage of business out there. If this deal doesn't fly, it isn't going to end my career or kill your future business.

Joanna Tamer

We don't know what the future will bring. We do have a chance to unfold our days one by one and piece together a story that shapes us. It's the only life anyone ever has. Hold on.

John Edgar Wideman

And You Can Succeed

Hard work, intelligence and discipline are the key ingredients of anyone's success. With them a person of any color can overcome practically any obstacle—and that includes discrimination, poverty, and almost any other condition that has nothing to do with your will to succeed.

Charles Barkley

If you can dream it, you can do it.

Walt Disney

Success is for those who want it and take action to get it.

Jim Brown

Successful people are intensely action-oriented.

Brian Tracy

It's not the cut of a man's coat, nor the manner of his dress. It's service that measures success.

George Washington Carver

If your goal is success, you must think of yourself as a success. You must expect success. You must feel deep down inside that you deserve success.

Wayne Allyn Root

Success is not the key to happiness. Happiness is the key to success. If you love what you are doing, you will be successful.

Herman Cain

The biggest fun of all is success. At the end of every day, every week, every quarter, it's fun to know you've done well.

Robert Shillman

Success is . . . about dreaming big dreams, setting specific goals and realizing them.

Darnell Sutton

If you can learn to THINK BIG, nothing on earth will keep you from being successful in whatever you choose to do.

Benjamin S. Carson, Sr.

Wanting something is not enough. You must hunger for it. Your motivation must be absolutely compelling in order to overcome the obstacles that will invariably come your way.

Les Brown

We give players everything to help them be successful today. . . . We provide everything except heart, desire and competitiveness. That you can't give a player.

Elgin Baylor

If you have the attitude of a winner, you will always win.

Dary Rees

Remember, money, position, power, and recognition are residual rewards of winning.

Pat Riley

Money is not the key. Money makes life easier, but money is not what gives you success. Integrity, dignity, self-respect; that is success.

Sinbad

The key to success in today's business environment is co-evolution—that is building links with others so that we all evolve and get stronger.

James Moore

One important key to success is self-confidence.
An important key to self-confidence is
preparation.

Arthur Ashe

The primary difference between success and
failure is proper preparation.

Kelvin Boston

That which we do to help others succeed aids our
own success.

Harold Washington

Once you've got success, it's empty. The fun is in
reaching for it.

Naomi Sims

Success is a journey, not a destination.

Deepak Chopra

Everyone is a person first and a success second.

Terrie Williams

You cannot be successful and continue to be a
victim.

Maxine Waters

Nothing succeeds like success.

Alexandre Dumas, *pere*

Success is the best revenge.

Vanessa Williams

Success can be defined as the progressive realization of worthy goals, . . . the fulfillment of our desires, . . . the progressive expansion of the state of happiness.

Deepak Chopra

If one advances confidently in the direction of his dreams, and endeavors to live the life which he has imagined, he will meet with success unexpected in common hours.

Henry David Thoreau

With Ability

I decided early in my career that the only really important thing was to try and win every game. . . . The only thing that really mattered was who won. There is nothing subjective about that.

Bill Russell

The plan begins with having the right attitude. Without that attitude most [people] will not attain the goal of wealth that they seek.

Brooke Stephens

I want to be remembered as a person who felt there was no limitation to what the human body and human mind can do and be the inspiration to lead people to do things they never hoped to do.

Carl Lewis

If you believe in your ability to succeed, you'll be more likely to do so.

Fran Harris

Even when I wasn't making any money, I *always* knew I was good.

Whoopi Goldberg

I knew if I came out here and played every day, I'd get into a rhythm, and I have.

Tiger Woods

When I played [football], I never doubted my ability and could look into the eyes of my teammates when the heat was really on and tell who could perform and who couldn't.

Reginald F. Lewis

Regardlesss of race, color or creed, we are all dealt a hand to play in this game of life. And believe me, Reg Lewis played the hell out of his hand.

Bill Cosby

We do what we can. And by our doing it, we help ourselves.

June Jordan

Accomplishments have no color.

Leontyne Price

When I walk into a room I assume I have to prove myself. I know that. I'm accustomed to that. But I also know I can prove myself.

Yvonne Brathwaite Burke

My goal is to make it more difficult for people to say "but. . . ."

Ron Brown

It's important that you have no sense of inferiority about what you're learning or about your abilities.

J. Bruce Llewellyn

What has fascinated me . . . has been the electricity of making a deal, the challenge of managing the human elements, and the adrenaline-flowing gamble of keeping nine or ten balls in the air.

John H. Johnson

What sets us apart is that like many other small businesses . . . we are on the cutting edge of our business.

Wade Hudson

Seeing me maintain my dignity in the struggle and stay strong gave [my daughters] the feeling that if there's something they want to do, they can do it—including running the family business.

Michele Hoskins

My grandfather said . . . "Always remember, your skill is what's important. Get that and build on it and sooner or later you'll have a big payday—count on it."

Reginald F. Lewis

No matter what you do in the world of business, you must have sharp listening skills.

Mary Kay Ash

Many of the traits that help people succeed in the entrepreneurial stage of a company become problematic in the long run. . . . You have to make adjustments as the company grows.

Richard Hagberg

We're not just about making money. We want to set an example that small businesses can lead the way.

Glynn Lloyd

Hard Work

If you work long and hard you will win the entrepreneurial race and become a huge business success.

Fran Harris

When you start off, you're [working] 24 hours a day. I don't care what anybody says—that's just what you do.

Rochelle Balch

There is no cure that does not cost.

Gikuyu proverb

A man's bread and butter is only insured when he works for it.

Marcus Garvey

You just have to keep the old garment-district-shirt-sleeves-up attitude towards work.

Melvin Van Peebles

I was pushing and driving people beyond their sense of what was possible.

> Berry Gordy

The good thing about hard work is that it brings more work.

> Donn Nettles

Hard work is good for a man. It's something he can do without thinking or worrying.

> Walter Mosley

I figure work is healthy, so I just keep doing it.

> Clint Eastwood

You can't talk your way out of problems you behave yourself into.

> Stephen R. Covey

All work is honorable. Always do your best, because someone is watching.

> Colin Powell

The quality of your work—and persistence— speak for themselves.

> Mary J. Cronin

Too many see what they don't have and want it all at once. . . . They have become . . . preoccupied with image instead of substance.

T. M. Alexander

Being good at anything . . . means devoting time, energy and effort. . . . My dream came true . . . but most of all it took a great deal of self-discipline.

Debi Thomas

A dream doesn't become reality through magic; it takes sweat, determination and hard work.

Colin Powell

I have always approached practice as a kind of proving ground, especially with rookies. They might have seen me on television, read about me . . . and might think they know what I'm all about. . . . I want them to know [it] isn't gossip or rumors. I want them to know it all comes from hard work.

Michael Jordan

You don't just get a work ethic. You've got to come with it.

Karl Malone

Anything in life worth having is worth working for.

Andrew Carnegie

As people come here [to Inner City Broadcasting Corporation] to participate in this dream . . . they have learned to work. . . . We come to share the dream, to work for it.

Percy Sutton

People who do well are not geniuses; they don't have a birthright for doing well. Somebody helped them along the way and they did the hard work along the way.

Deborah Prothrow-Stith

It's hard work that separates so-called geniuses from the also-rans.

Abdulalim Shabazz

No matter what you may or may not have, . . . people understand hard work and talent—and it can prevail.

Maxine Waters

We are in the business of exceeding people's expectations.

Michael Eisner

You just have to choose your weapons. I chose the ones my mother gave me: love, dignity and hard work.

Gordon Parks

To be good at anything—be it in sports, school or being somebody's friend—it takes a great deal of work, concentration and sacrifice.

Walter Payton

When I went to the playground I never picked the best players. I picked guys with less talent, but who were willing to work hard, who had the desire to be great.

Magic Johnson

It is so important to always be prospecting for new business, no matter how busy you are.

Danielle Kennedy

The best way to make a go of a seasonal business is to treat it like a year-round venture.

Roberta Maynard

Stay on top of what's happening in your industry.

Robert Imbriale

One philosophy that has stood me well is that I never turn down a job. As a result, I've grown rapidly, and we've catered as many as five affairs on the same night.

Norma Jean Darden

Everything you deserve will eventually come your way. You won't have to grab for it. You won't have to force it. It will simply catch up to you, drawn along in the jetstream, the forward motion of your hard work.

Pat Riley

If you fall in love with what you do, you never work again.

John H. Johnson

Cooperation

Competition as we have known it, the head-to-head conflicts of the past, is no longer the way to build a business.

James Moore

Letting go is tough for an entrepreneur, but it's an essential step in growing a business.

Christopher Hegarty

When you get right down to it, and when all is said and done, it is how you connect with people on a human, personal level that will ensure your success.

Terrie Williams

I think that those of us who have been fortunate enough to gain the contacts should reach out to help true entrepreneurs with financing and the know-how to build significant businesses that can employ large numbers of people.

Jesse Hill, Jr.

When I came to this country, I was helped to get where I am. I always felt I had an obligation to help people, too.

Alexander Torimiro

Always be prepared to network.

George Fraser

Part of networking is learning how to get into the system as well as learning what kind of skills are needed.

Alvin Poussaint

The morality and consciousness of people under capitalism tends to be individualistic.

Amiri Baraka

Interdependence is a higher value than independence, [but] effective interdependence can only be built on a foundation of true independence.

Stephen R. Covey

No one, black or white, succeeds on his own; you have to be part of a network.

Tony Brown

There are tremendous opportunities for finding a profitable place in a fast-evolving global economy if the entrepreneur understands that he or she is not alone.

James Moore

Always surround yourself with good, solid professionals.

Terrie Williams

[Our best business move was] forming a board of directors that includes experienced professionals. We don't know it all, and their advice has been priceless.

Carole J. Gellineau

Business is people. . . . You don't make it happen, people make it happen.

J. Bruce Llewellyn

In every contact with a person, give them something they will value.

Adriane Berg

The only networking that works is networking for the benefit of others.

George Fraser

A loud voice is not always angry; a soft voice not always to be dismissed; and a well-placed silence can be the indisputable last word.

Gloria Naylor

A close friend can become a close enemy.

Ethiopian proverb

Colors and labels have a way of categorizing people and creating artificial constraints around people and the way they think about themselves.

Reginald F. Lewis

It's always important to keep in mind the interchange that goes on even as we avoid one another.

Ralph W. Ellison

Social identities are never as rigid as we like to pretend: they're constantly being contested and negotiated.

Henry Louis Gates, Jr.

I think we'd all be amazed at what simple conversation, truly held, can achieve in human relationships.

Ossie Davis

Everybody in the world wants the same thing. . . .
to be needed . . . a job that he/she can do
well . . . to love somebody. . . . Everybody.
There's no mystery.

Maya Angelou

Everybody's negotiable.

Muhammad Ali

While many people think of networks as
business tools, they have historically been
used to implement social change.

George Fraser

I just don't believe there is any higher calling for a
talented business person these days than to tackle
the job of developing our communities.

Jesse Hill, Jr.

We see [changing the environment of inner
cities] more as a commitment to doing things that
make economic sense for poor people.

Egbert Perry

People don't care about you until they realize
how much you care about them.

Dennis Kimbro

Amazing things happen when you're nice to
people others overlook.

Terrie Williams

By giving first, you stand out in people's minds,
and they want to do business with you.

Adriane Berg

Everyone wants to be appreciated, so if you
appreciate someone, don't keep it a secret.

Mary Kay Ash

The key to working with a performer is
remembering this person is a human being
[with] gifts. Love and respect force you to pay
attention to all the intricacies of those gifts.

Quincy Jones

I want [my children] to realize that you don't have
to stab anybody in the back. You don't have to
scratch anybody's eyes out. Just be honest, work
hard and have faith. That will take them further
in life than anything.

Denzel Washington

Real strength entails being considerate and
supportive of people's feelings.

Mary Kay Ash

What appealed to me about the [triangle offense] system was that it empowered everybody on the team by making them more involved in the offense and demanded that they put their individual needs second to those of the group.

Phil Jackson

From space, you see earth and earthlings the way God sees us. . . . as one people, unified, working together.

Bernard Harris

When spiderwebs unite, they can tie up a lion.

Ethiopian proverb

United we stand, divided we fall.

Aesop

. . . We are each other's
harvest:
we are each other's
business:
we are each other's
magnitude and bond.

Gwendolyn Brooks in "Paul Robeson"

Perseverance

When you suffer something like that defeat . . . one of two things is going to happen. You are going to learn from that experience or you're going to crumble beneath the memory. We had the right kind of character to not give up. [That] prepared us to be champions.

Joe Dumars

Losing is not the *opposite* of winning; it is often just a step away from total victory. . . . To quit before a full commitment is made is to throw away all your previous lessons and efforts without any hope of a return. Quitting . . . can become habit forming.

George Subira

Fail enough, and you will eventually fail your way to the top.

Wayne Allyn Root

Never give in, never give in, never, never, never, never—in nothing, great or small, large or petty— never give in except to convictions of honor and good sense.

Winston Churchill

Do not give up too early on the deals you really want. . . . Fail to follow through, and you're showing them you don't care. Follow through, and you just may get the biggest deal of your life.

Danielle Kennedy

Do not give up, and always create your own momentum. . . . Build on every success to get more successes. And never quit.

Mark Victor Hansen

I look around and see people who are so ready to give up and I tell them, "Study harder, work harder."

Martha Dixon

Tenacity and perseverance are essential qualities for success in business.

Mary Kay Ash

The ability to stay on a task until it is accomplished is a prerequisite. You must fight the boredom and other distracting elements. Staying on task is essential.

Alvin Foster

You can win if you got the heart and tenacity and soul to keep on trying.

Miles Davis

If something doesn't work, don't give up, go a different direction.

Edward G. Gardner

There's something much more important than goals, and that's having the commitment and the passion to stick with your goals.

Wayne Allyn Root

Persistence is one of the keys to the kingdom.

Spike Lee

I think that mental and physical agility is necessary to endure, for they provide a balance and demonstrate the unlimited energy or potential within us.

Paul Goodnight

Heart can take you far. If you don't have it, you don't have a chance.

Dennis Rodman

He who starts behind in the great race of life must forever remain behind or run faster than the man in front.

Benjamin E. Mays

I don't think there are any shortcuts to achievement. I go slowly, if necessary, and pay a lot of attention to the community around me.

T. M. Alexander

I believe we should extend our time lines and give ourselves a little more time to be successful.

Adriane Berg

Nothing is possible without patience.

Chin-Ning Chu

Doing [marketing] right requires commitment, patience and planning. Expect miracles and you'll get ulcers.

Jay Conrad Levinson

I'm able to tell kids if there's something that they like or something that they've dreamed about, it doesn't matter what their situation is. With perseverance, it [can] be done.

Robin Petgrave

The more you do it right, the more likely you are to *keep* doing it right. The next time you do [the right thing], it is much easier.

Ralph Warner

A great accomplishment takes a lot of perseverance. If you study achievers throughout history, you'll learn that their successes did not come easily.

Mary Kay Ash

Perseverance is my motto.

Madame C. J. Walker

Patience and persistence . . . alone solve real problems.

Booker T. Washington

Nothing in the world can take the place of persistence. Talent will not; nothing is more common than unsuccessful men with talent. Genius will not; unregarded genius is almost a proverb. Education will not; the world is full of educated derelicts. Persistence and determination alone are omnipotent.

Calvin Coolidge

We will not sprint to victory. Rather, we are long-distance runners in a relay race. We have come too far to be side-tracked or detoured or to get weak in the knees and not go the distance.

Susan L. Taylor

It's not over until you win.

Les Brown

Marketing

Not having a marketing plan in place for your business will be one of the biggest obstacles to your success.

Cheryl D. Broussard

Guerrilla marketers . . . know marketing isn't costly, but marketing mistakes are.

Jay Conrad Levinson

You've got to let people know you're in business if you want to make any money.

Diane Shelton

Marketing is about being remembered.

Lynn Beresford

Think of marketing as sell business, as create-a-desire business, as motivation business. . . .
Marketing is not supposed to entertain.

Jay Conrad Levinson

[We] believed strongly that all we had to do was make good products and the orders would come . . . We had a lesson to learn. . . . To sell our tapecorder we would have to identify the people and institutions that would be likely to recognize value in our product.

Akio Morita

Just because people say no today doesn't mean they won't be saying yes tomorrow—if you rethink how you are marketing your service.

Mark Victor Hansen

Marketing yourself is one of the most important ways to get ahead in this world, whether it be in college, at work, or in your personal life.

Terrie Williams

As a marketer, trend knowledge is invaluable. To be where the consumers are just before they get there, offering these consumers what they didn't know they wanted, spells success.

Faith Popcorn

Eventually everyone will be buying, selling and marketing over the airwaves and cyberspace.

Pedro Alfonso

Misguided business owners think marketing is over once they've made the sale. Wrong! Marketing *begins* once you've made the sale.

Jay Conrad Levinson

Consumers are infinitely wiser about the ways of marketing than they used to be.

Ross E. Goldstein

I take a very direct approach to [marketing]. I like to peel away the layers of the onion and get to the core of each marketplace I want to reach.

Marsha Feltingoff

All effective advertising is aimed at segments of the market, not a general market.

Thomas J. Burrell

It's a misconception to talk about the marketplace in any kind of general, grand way. You have to talk about specific corners of the marketplace.

Ross E. Goldstein

In the international marketplace now taking
shape, acting locally but thinking globally will be
the key to economic growth.

Ron Watkins

To operate internationally, you have to have a lot
of patience.

Harold Jackson

[The ethnic consumer markets are] unmined
gold. The income they represent is well above
the income potential of certain countries in the
world, including Canada.

Amy Hilliard-Jones

There are bounded markets—the entrepreneur
just has to learn to look for them.

James Moore

The challenge for us is being creative, developing
new markets and convincing prospective clients
[to buy our products].

Ernesta Procope

The only way to market to people is to create
your marketing as if you are talking to one
individual rather than to a group.

Phil Goodman

I know it sounds warm and fuzzy, but if you have good relationships with consumers, your market will grow.

Ivan Burwell

For years we had shown the world what we could do with talent and ingenuity as our base. Now these new corporate entities were showing me what they could do with money and power as theirs.

Berry Gordy

There are over 100 weapons of marketing out there. Advertising is one of them.

Jay Conrad Levinson

Word-of-mouth . . . is incredibly effective if your product is genuinely better than anyone else's.

Peter Adkison

Say what you will do loud and clear. Do it better than anybody else and then remind people to death about how well you did it.

Joshua I. Smith

Sales and Service

Build rapport, don't sell.

George Fraser

One of the first lessons in selling is, make it easy for the buyer to buy.

Lou Pritchett

In the world of business, and especially in selling, rejection comes with the territory.

Mary Kay Ash

Don't let a perceived disadvantage stop your sales. Turn the negative into a positive, and you will close your deals.

Tom Hopkins

At the moment of a major decision, there's always hesitation. The professional salesperson has to find a way to nudge the prospect past that point.

Brian Tracy

The ability to relate successfully with people turns contacts into contracts.

Terrie Williams

The processes involved in selling are fairly standard, no matter what is being sold. . . . Once a person has learned the sales process, cold, they are . . . in a position to sell just about anything.

George Subira

In business, you are only as successful as the options you have for selling.

Brian Tracy

He who sells not can buy not.

W. Edwards Deming

Surround yourself with positive people—other entrepreneurs or salespeople who are really good at cold calls.

Danielle Kennedy

I call selling myself "peacocking."

Wardell Sullivan

I believe that the most commercial element in music, no matter what the genre, is sincerity, that you really believe in what you're doing.

Quincy Jones

We built our customer list from our memberships in several organizations and later bought a mailing list to enhance our customer base.

Jennifer Clark

You'd better be on top of what it is your customers value and continually improve your offerings to better deliver that value.

Jill Griffin

I thought I could provide a better service to customers than the larger companies, who were more concerned with just the bottom line.

Margie Lewis

To win in the industrial world, you need customers who believe in you.

Dave Bing

Stay in the face of your customers to make sure they're happy.

Dorothy J. White

All customers are not created equal. Some of them have buying habits and buying behaviors that are far more valuable to a [business]. The key is looking at the long-term potential of each customer segment.

Jill Griffin

An ongoing relationship with customers is a great thing from a business point of view.

Bill Gates

Our proudest achievement is the ability to sustain continuing relationships with clients and to build up their confidence so that . . . they continue with us.

Martha Rothman

Even if we lost money on the transaction, we wanted a customer who loved us at the end of the day.

Steve Leveen

For good value and exceptional service, [your customers] will reward you with repeat business and by referring additional customers to you.

Mary Kay Ash

I think our success has to do not only with the quality of our food, but also with how we treat people.

T. J. Robinson

Treat people with respect and be an honorable human being and you'll end up a winner.

Grant Hill

America doesn't understand that real service means being servile—to take a subservient position with the customer, to obey without question.

Evelyn Echols

Bad guys get all the press, but being a good guy is the real way to get wealthy.

Milton Gralla

I've found that you can deal fairly with people and make a lot of money at the same time.

Dempsey Travis

I thought if you could actually put out a product that people wanted to buy and that could change things, that would be much more powerful than . . . lecturing the world.

Ralph Warner

In life and business, your name is all you've got to trade on.

Harvey Mackay

In the long run, your reputation is what you have to uphold.

Jennifer Kraljevich

Really good companies are creating a brand image both for their products and for the way they deal with customers. That's very powerful.

Richard C. Whiteley

Listen more. Ask more questions. Talk less. You find out amazing things about customers when you listen.

Danielle Kennedy

When building a new business . . . have a relationship with customers where they will tell you what they do and don't like.

James Moore

I like to think of my customers as just an extension of my business and they think that way, too.

Edwin C. Laird

[We stay hungry because] we never waste time talking about what we're doing well. It just isn't our culture. Every meeting is about "Sure, we won in seven of the categories, but what about that eighth category?"

Bill Gates

[Entrepreneurs] need to constantly reassess every aspect of their businesses . . . to come up with products and services nobody else can offer, in ways that are increasingly efficient.

Geoffrey Kessler

We have to develop businesses that provide products and services that companies choose to buy.

William G. Mays

You've got to be competitive. If you're not willing to be competitive, you're not going to make it.

J. Bruce Llewellyn

Everything rests on our ability to produce quality products for our customers. That's the ballgame. . . . And that quality . . . depends on that worker on the floor.

Aaron Feuerstein

There's absolutely no limit to what plain, ordinary working people can accomplish if they're given the opportunity, the encouragement and the incentive to do their best.

Sam Walton

I give [my employees] the freedom to develop the strategies necessary to get the job done.

Drew Pearson

The individual is the Digital Economy's basic unit of wealth creation.

Don Tapscott

What is going to separate you or your company from competitors with the same capabilities and skills? You need something more. You need a personal touch.

Terrie Williams

And Make Lots of Money

The way to cure poverty is with money. And the way to generate that in a community is with business.

Bob Johnson

The banker's ethic to the contrary, few people in the normal economy grow rich or even affluent through the simple process of faithfully and periodically depositing money in a savings account.

Theodore L. Cross

How one makes money is as important as how much one makes.

Shelley Green and Paul Pryde

The only limit on your income is you.

Dennis Kimbro and Napoleon Hill

I realized it was a mind-set, how much money you make.

Lorraine Miller

A man ought to get all he can earn. A man who knows he's making money for other people ought to get some of the profit he brings in. Don't make any difference if it's baseball or a bank or a vaudeville show.

Babe Ruth

The real question isn't if I'm worth $120 million; it's, if somebody can afford to pay me $120 million, how much is *he* making?

Shaquille O'Neal

It's not what you're worth, it's what you can negotiate.

John Salley

Money makes me happy. . . . I long ago decided that, on the whole, I much prefer having money to not having it. In that sense, it makes me happy.

Arthur Ashe

Our aim is to have a lot of fun making a lot of money.

Robert Shillman

Everyone has the same objective—to end up with more dough than they start with at a minimum of risk.

Warren Buffett

Money never has meant that much to me, not even in the sense of keeping score.

Sam Walton

I don't like money actually, but it quiets my nerves.

Joe Louis

Politics don't control the world, money does.

Andrew Young

I've *arranged* my life so that I can do what I want.

Warren Buffett

That's really what wealth does for you. It gives you freedom to make choices.

Oprah Winfrey

Football is still #1 for me. It's got to be #1. It's making me more money.

Deion Sanders

It's not the gold I want; it's the green.

Carl Lewis

I don't play this game for money. People come out to watch you play, not to count your money.

Kevin Garnett

I like to put meaningful amounts of money in a few things.

Warren Buffett

You have to pay for fame—mentally, spiritually, and in *real* money.

Miles Davis

Since when did money become life?

Lorraine Hansberry

Money will never change my attitude toward life. Don't get me wrong, I enjoy having it, but it's not going to make me foolish.

Leonard Sanders

There is hardly any money interest in the realm of art, [but] music will be here when money is gone.

Louis Armstrong

I've never understood how people can make money rapping, but they do and I cannot knock success.

Pervis Spann

The bottom line is, is it commercial? Is everybody else gonna like it?

Kenneth "Babyface" Edmonds

I make movies because I like movies, but I found out that not everybody in the business likes movies. They're making movies because they like money.

John Singleton

My hope is to create high-quality products that enhance people's lives. The money is just a byproduct.

Andrew Zenoff

I don't think you can achieve wealth if you're trying to get wealthy. It comes from service and achievement.

John H. Johnson

Money, it turned out, was exactly like sex, you thought of nothing else if you didn't have it and thought of other things if you did.

James Baldwin

Money, like sex, is one of those loaded issues that frequently compels lies, exaggerations, half truths, and some degree of guilt.

Audrey Edwards and Craig K. Polite

[In this country, the attitude toward money is this]: Get what you can. Can what you get and sit on the can.

Pat Schroeder

There's a big difference between writing a check and managing money.

B. Denise Owens

Money is a great dignifier.

Paul Laurence Dunbar

The fate of small businesses will always be linked to their ability to raise capital.

Matthew S. Scott and Carolyn M. Brown

Capital is very hard to come by, . . . but my
background is Wall Street; raising capital is like
mother's milk to me.

Don Cornwell

Getting money isn't easy, but in the quest for
expansion capital, overeager entrepreneurs often
miss some obvious, telltale warning signs.

Brian Steinberg

It's amazing how many entrepreneurs will hire
someone to help them raise money without ever
checking to see that they have successfully done it
before.

Barry Suskind

When it comes to raising money, haste can land
you in a lot of hot water. . . . There is a certain
maturation process that has to take place.
Growing overnight can lead to significant pain
and discomfort.

Mark Griffin

Commercial banks lend most freely to those who
possess significant amounts of equity capital to
invest in their businesses.

Timothy Bates

Banks have changed. [They] are targeting small businesses with innovative programs and increased vigor.

Rieva Lesonsky

We [financed the business] our way. It gave us a little more flexibility.

Lamont Kennerly

[Financing the film *Get On the Bus*] was a great opportunity for us to raise the money ourselves. . . . A lot of it had to do with self-empowerment.

Spike Lee

We see manufacturing as a means to mobilize resources . . . a way to reach beyond boundaries and pull in dollars from outside. That's how you really build wealth.

Roy Terry

For the record, *profits* is not a dirty word. It's just that it should not be the only priority.

Mary Kay Ash

Enough to Give Some Away

It's possible an entrepreneur's moral choices may cost the company money. If that weren't true, there would be nothing particularly wonderful about people who make moral choices.

John Tepper Marlin

When [Southwest Airlines] is challenged and tested, it always comes down on the side of what's good for people. Even if the costs are significant.

Kevin Freiberg and Jackie Freiberg

For a businessman to give back to the community, it helps to have a successful business.

Tony March

I felt that I had to make it in business so I could help somebody else.

Lee McCord

The way we look at it, we want to give something back. . . . It's an extra motivation to work harder for our success.

John W. Rogers, Jr.

My object in life is not simply to make money for myself or to spend it on myself. I love to use a part of what I make in trying to help others.

Madame C. J. Walker

Of course I make money. Money is neutral; it's what you do with it. I'm worth nothing. I've given all my money away. And when I make money from [The House of Blues], I'll give that away, too.

Isaac Tigrett

I want to share the wealth. My goal is to continue helping people through my products.

Jill Nadine Clements

You can only use so much money for yourself. . . . The rest of the money we want to do a lot of things to return to the community, the people, who have made this possible.

John Tu

Give until it hurts and then give until it feels good.

George Fraser

If you do right, right will follow [you].

Oprah Winfrey

Once I stopped dwelling on what I *didn't* have, on what I thought I was going to lose, and began to give freely, everything began to flow into my life.

Patti LaBelle

Be prudent in your generosity. In fact, although charity is important, dispense with generosity if you must; deal first with your primary responsibilities.

Arthur Ashe

With every dollar you save a dime, you spend a quarter or fifty cents, and you give some of it away. To me, that's a spiritual use of money.

Margaret Walker Alexander

Man cannot live by profit alone.

James Baldwin

The man who dies rich, dies disgraced.

Andrew Carnegie

I don't think our democracy can survive if too many people fall through the cracks and don't enjoy its fruits.

Anthony Drexel Duke

Millions of white children of all classes, like too
many minority children, are drowning in the
meaninglessness of a culture that rewards greed
and guile and tells them life is about getting
rather than giving.

Marian Wright Edelman

Charitable works can show your intention to
make a positive contribution to the community
where you intend to establish your business.
Giving back . . . can open up many doors "at the
top" of political and business communities.

Ron Watkins

It's not a question of age or how much money you
have; you have to get in the habit of [giving money
away] like [you get in the habit of] brushing your
teeth.

Ted Turner

You can never give too much: that's something
[my mother] taught me when I was very young.

Steve Smith

What's interesting about subscribing to a life of
giving is that you become addicted.

Mary Kay Ash

Live on the give, not on the take, and you will get rich and stay rich.

Milton Gralla

There's real power in generosity.

Andre Harrell

I have not allowed my troubles to keep me from being involved. I believe that good things happened because I continued to give.

Wally "Famous" Amos

You can only receive what you're willing to give.

Pat Riley

[I gave away most of my money because] I simply decided I had enough money. It doesn't drive my life.

Charles F. Feeney

We make a living by what we get. We make a life by what we give.

Winston Churchill

I can't think of anything better you can do with large amounts of money [than use it to help others.]

Michael Bloomberg

When wealth is centralized, the people are dispersed. When wealth is distributed, the people are brought together.

Confucius

There's a higher good than "giving back" to the community; it is refusing to back out of the community; it is sharing the joys of success with as many people as possible.

Dale Dauten

The greatest thing a person can do is contribute to the well-being of another.

Jim Brown

Philanthropy has to be a part of your life. I always try to think of what I can do to make other people's lives a little easier, a little more comfortable.

Edward G. Gardner

Give more than your money. Give your time, heart, soul.

Kevin Freiberg and Jackie Freiberg

In war, we offer our very lives as a matter of routine. We must be no less daring, no less steadfast, in the pursuit of peace.

Jimmy Carter

About the Persons Quoted

A

Bella Abzug (75), a lawyer, is a former member of the U.S. Congress from New York. In 1990, she founded the nonprofit group WEDO (Women Environment and Development Organization) for the education, development, and visibility of women in society, from the local to the international level.

Chinua Achebe (65), a Nigerian writer and professor, has published a number of books for both adults and children, including *No Longer at Ease, The Sacrificial Egg and Other Stories, Arrow of God, A Man of the People, Christmas in Biafra and Other Poems, Flute,* and *The Drum.* His first novel, *Things Fall Apart,* was awarded the Margaret Wong Memorial Prize in 1959, and his *The Anthills of the Savannah* was nominated for the Booker Prize in England in 1987. He has also received the Nigerian National Trophy, the Jock Campbell/*New Statesman* Award, and the Nigerian National Merit Award.

Abigail Adams (47), 1744–1818, is best known for the letters she wrote to her husband John Adams, the second president of the United States, advising him on policy. Two volumes of her letters were published posthumously by their grandson, Charles Adams.

Peter Adkison (120) is the creator (with his partner Richard Garfield) of the top-selling card-collecting, role-playing game, *Magic: The Gathering.* Launched in 1993, the game has captured a $50 million share of the game market.

Aesop (19, 41, 47, 109), 620–560 B.C. is the Ethiopian writer who lived in Greece and authored *Aesop's Fables.*

African proverb (84) Information not available on specific source.

Akan proverb (50, 53) The Akan region consists of several ethnic groups in southern Ghana in West Africa.

Margaret Walker Alexander (139), an acclaimed writer whose works include *Jubilee* and *Richard Wright: Daemonic Genius,* received the Yale Series of Younger Poets Award in 1942 for her popular collection of poems *For My People.* She has also received Ford and Rosenthal fellowships.

T. M. Alexander (99, 113) is the founder of Alexander and Company, an insurance business in Atlanta, and author of *The Demise of Service: The Birth of Greed.*

Pedro Alfonso (118) is cofounder (with Benjamin Peasant), president, and chief executive officer (CEO) of Dynamic Concepts, Inc., based in Washington, D.C. The company (founded in 1979) uses optical disks to convert hard-copy documents into personal-computer files. Sales in 1993 were $20 million.

Muhammad Ali (5, 16, 47, 107) (né Cassius Clay) won an Olympic gold medal in boxing in 1960. Ali was the world heavyweight boxing champion an unprecedented three times and has often been called the most recognized person in the world. In 1977, he starred in a movie about his life, *The Greatest.*

Debbie Allen (79) won three Emmys for choreography on the hit television series *Fame.* She produced and directed *A Different World,* another long-running television series, and starred in *In the House.* In the world of film, she has appeared in *Ragtime, The Fish That Saved Pittsburgh,* and *Fame,* and she choreographed the Academy Awards for several years. Allen began her career as a dancer.

Kathleen R. Allen (31, 35) is a professor of entrepreneurship at the University of Southern California in Los Angeles and the author of *Launching New Ventures.*

Wally ("Famous") Amos (14, 37, 40, 59, 141) was the first person to establish stores devoted solely to selling cookies; his new business is The Uncle Noname Cookie Company. Amos works with the Cities in Schools program in Hawaii, where he lives and is a national spokesperson for Literacy Volunteers of America. He is also the author (with Stu Gluberman) of *Watermelon Magic*.

Eloise Anderson (4) is the director of California's welfare system, the largest welfare system in the country, with a caseload of 5 million.

Beverley Anderson-Manley (71) is cohost of *The Breakfast Club*, a television show in Jamaica, West Indies.

Maya Angelou (33, 66, 107) wrote "On the Pulse of the Morning," a poem commissioned by President Clinton for his 1993 inauguration. She also authored *I Know Why the Caged Bird Sings*, an autobiography nominated for a National Book Award; *Give Me A Cool Drink of Water 'fore I Diiie*, a volume of poetry nominated for a Pulitzer Prize; *Gather Together in My Name; And Still I Rise; Wouldn't Take Nothing for My Journey Now;* and several other books. Angelou, also an actress, has appeared in a number of film and television movies.

Lupe Anguiano (38) is the founder and president of National Women's Employment and Education, Inc.

Daniel Louis ("Satchmo") Armstrong (132), 1900–1971, was a jazz trumpet player and bandleader whose improvisational style influenced jazz musicians around the world. Armstrong appeared in a number of films and, after World War II, he often traveled overseas as a goodwill ambassador for the United States.

Mary Kay Ash (38, 55, 70, 96, 108, 111, 114, 121, 124, 136, 140) was a single mother with three children when she started Mary Kay Cosmetics, Inc., which employs 400,000 independent beauty consultants. Ash is currently chair emeritus of her $1.5 billion company and the author of *Mary Kay: You Can Have It All*.

Ashanti proverb (33, 47) Ashanti are a people residing primarily in Ghana in West Africa.

Arthur Ashe (40, 91, 130, 139), 1943–1993, was the first African American player named to the American Davis Cup team. In addition to tennis championships won in college, he was the American clay-court champion in 1967 and the first African American male to win the singles title at Wimbledon.

He later became captain of the Davis Cup team and authored the four-volume history of sports, *A Hard Road to Glory*.

Anne Ashmore (38) is a psychologist in private practice in Brookline, Massachusetts.

Augustine (5, 52) (Saint) of Hippo, 354–430, was a philosopher and a bishop. Through his well-known works *The City of God* and *Confessions*, he had a profound impact on the Christian world.

B

Allan Bailey (50) is the executive director of San Diego State University's Entrepreneurial Management Center.

Pearl Bailey (15), 1918–1990, got started in the entertainment business after she won first place at an amateur night at the Apollo Theater. During her long career, she was a dancer, singer, and actress, appearing in several films, including *Carmen Jones, St. Louis Blues,* and *Porgy and Bess.* She also authored *The Raw Pearl, Hurry Up America and Spit,* and other books.

Anita Baker (74), a vocalist, has won seven Grammy Awards, selling more than 11 million copies of her first four albums in the United States alone. She and her husband, Walter Bridgforth, have financial holdings in excess of $4 million. They have established the Bridgforth Foundation, providing scholarship money for students at a Detroit elementary school Baker "adopted."

Rochelle Balch (17, 97) is the owner of RB Balch & Associates, a computer consulting firm in Glendale, Arizona, and winner of the 1996 Entrepreneurial Woman Home-Based Business of the Year.

James Baldwin (134, 139), 1924–1987, was one of the finest essayists of the twentieth century. He also wrote short stories, plays, and novels. In 1948, he received a Rosenwald Fellowship, which enabled him to move to Paris where he completed his first novel, *Go Tell It on the Mountain.* His other novels include *Another Country, Giovanni's Room,* and *Just Above My Head.* Among Baldwin's essay collections are *Nobody Knows My Name, The Fire Next Time,* and *The Evidence of Things Not Seen.*

Amiri Baraka (52, 104) (né LeRoi Jones) has been a community leader in New Ark, (Newark) New Jersey, for many years. He is also a prolific writer of poetry, fiction, and drama. His publications include *Preface to a Twenty Volume Suicide Note, Spirit Reach, The System of Dante's Hell, Blues People, Black Music, Dutchman, The Slave, Four Black Revolutionary Plays,* and many others.

Don Barden (22) is the chair and CEO of Barden Communications, Inc., in Detroit, Michigan.

Charles Barkley (18, 78, 88) has been named an All-Star player eleven times in the National Basketball Association (NBA) and won two Olympic gold medals. He was named one of the fifty greatest players in the history of the NBA.

Sandra Williams Bate (44) is the owner of Bate's Motor Home Rental Network in Las Vegas.

Daisy Bates (19) (with her husband, L. C. Bates) owned the *Arkansas State Press,* which they used to advocate for racial justice. She was pivotal in the desegregation of Central High School in Little Rock in 1957, about which she writes in *The Long Shadow of Little Rock.*

Timothy Bates (135) is a professor of labor and urban affairs at Wayne State University in Detroit.

Elgin Baylor (90) played professional basketball with the Los Angeles Lakers. He was named one of the fifty greatest players in the history of the NBA.

Ella L. J. Edmondson Bell (2, 73) is a professor of organizational management at the University of North Carolina at Charlotte.

Janet Cheatham Bell (24, 28, 45), the author of this collection, is described in "About the Author," on the last page of this book.

Ronald Berenbeim (11, 12) is a senior research associate of The Conference Board in New York City, a business membership and research organization.

Lynn Beresford (116) is a staff writer for *Entrepreneur,* a magazine for small businesses.

Adriane G. Berg (105, 108, 113) publishes a financial newsletter and hosts *The Money Show* on WABC in New York City. She is also co-author (with Milton Gralla) of *How Good Guys Grow Rich.*

John Bernard (26), a fashion designer, founded (in 1986) and owns Spot International, which anticipated revenues of $30 million in 1996.

Mary McLeod Bethune (87), 1875–1955, was the director of the National Business League; the founder and former president (until 1947) of Bethune-Cookman College in Daytona Beach, Florida; and the founder-president of the National Council of Negro Women. She was also the first African American woman to head a federal office, the Division of Negro Affairs of the National Youth Administration, under President Franklin Roosevelt.

Dave Bing (123) is the founder and CEO of The Bing Group, Inc., which manufactures automotive parts. All of Bing's businesses are located within the city of Detroit. He is a former professional basketball player for the Detroit Pistons and was selected as one of the fifty greatest players in the history of the NBA.

Julie Blau (57, 58) is co-author (with Bryan Drysdale) of *Problem Solving for Entrepreneurs: A Creative New Approach to Overcoming Your Business Problems.*

Michael Bloomberg (141) is a former bond trader who has built a media empire that provides financial services, information, and news. He is the author of *Bloomberg by Bloomberg.*

Kelvin Boston (11, 12, 25, 91) is the host of the television show *The Color of Money* and the author of *Smart Money Moves for African Americans.*

Sy Bounds (63) has joined with others to host seminars teaching architectural rehabilitaion ("rehabbing") and entrepreneurial skills to his neighbors in the inner city. He is a painting and rehab contractor in Oak Park, Illinois, who participated in the Million Man March.

Barbara Landers Bowles (75) is the CEO of The Kenwood Group, an investment company in Chicago.

Melissa Bradley (64) is founder and executive director of The Entrepreneurial Development Institute, based in Washington, D.C.

Gwendolyn Brooks (41, 109) is Poet Laureate of the State of Illinois and was the Poetry Consultant to the Library of Congress in 1985–1986. She is the author of several books of poetry, including *Winnie, To Disembark, In the Mecca,* and *Annie Allen,* for which she received a Pulitzer Prize in 1950, becoming the first African American to break that barrier.

Joanne Brooks (36) is president of the Creative Impact Group, Inc., in Deerfield, Illinois.

Pauline C. Brooks (22) is CEO and president of Management Technology, Inc., of Clinton, Maryland, which has eight branches nationwide and more than $25 million in annual sales revenues. She was named the 1995 Woman-Owned Business Entrepreneur of the Year by Ernst & Young.

Cheryl D. Broussard (27, 42, 116) is the author of *Sister CEO: The Black Woman's Guide to Starting Your Own Business.* She also wrote *The Black Woman's Guide to Financial Independence: Smart Ways to Take Charge of Your Money, Build Wealth and Achieve Financial Security.*

Carolyn M. Brown (134) is a senior editor for *Black Enterprise,* a magazine that supports and encourages the business aspirations of African Americans.

Jim Brown (88, 142) is the founder and president of Amer-I-Can, an organization that helps inmates, ex-convicts, and gang members to turn their lives around. Brown's program has trained 17,000 inmates in California and more than 4,000 in New Jersey, and it has a presence in 24 schools in Ohio. He was a record-setting professional football player for the Cleveland Browns from 1957 to 1965. He is also a movie actor.

Les Brown (55, 84, 90, 115) is a nationally known motivational speaker and author of *Live Your Dreams* and *It's Not Over Until You Win.*

Ronald H. ("Ron") Brown (95), 1941–1996, was U.S. Secretary of Commerce when he died leading a trade mission in Europe. He had been deputy campaign manager for Senator Edward Kennedy's presidential run in 1979, a corporate lobbyist, and in 1989 became the first African American to head the Democratic National Committee.

Tony Brown (104) is the star of the television show *Tony Brown's Journal* and an avid promoter of entrepreneurship. He is also the author of *No More White Lies, No More Black Lies, Only the Truth.*

Dorothy Brunson (64, 71, 72, 73) is the founder, owner, and CEO of Brunson Communications, Inc., which comprises various independent television stations headquartered in Baltimore, with sales of $5 million. By the year 2000, Brunson hopes to own fifteen television stations

John H. Bryan (76) chairs Catalyst, a women's advocacy group. He also chairs the Sara Lee Corporation, an $18 billion company that is a leading global manufacturer and marketer of high-quality brand-name products.

Warren Buffett (131, 132) uses a "buy-and-hold" investment strategy, which has resulted in his having a net worth over $10 billion. His current holdings include major shares in the Walt Disney Company, the Gannett Company, and American Express.

Ralph J. Bunche (59), 1904–1971, was a diplomat perhaps best known for heading the delegation that brought temporary peace to the Arab–Israeli conflict in 1948. He began his government service in 1941 with the Office of Strategic Services and later joined the U.S. Department of State. In 1968, he was Undersecretary General of the United Nations.

Yvonne Brathwaite Burke (95) is a specialist in public finance and partner in a law firm. In 1972, she became the first woman of African descent elected to the U.S. Congress from the state of California.

Thomas J. Burrell (118) is the founder and CEO of Burrell Communications Group, which has offices in Chicago, Atlanta, and New York, with annual billings of $115 million.

Ivan Burwell (120) works in the Community Relations Department and is the national program manager for Coors Brewing Company.

Octavia Butler (24) has received the Hugo Award, the Nebula Award, and the Locus Award for her science-fiction writing. She is the author of *Bloodchild, Patternmaster, Wild Seed,*

Parable of the Sower, Kindred, and other science-fiction novels.

Bill Bygrave (20) is the director of the Center for Entrepreneurial Studies at Babson College in Wellesley, Massachusetts.

C

Herman Cain (12, 89) led an executive team in the purchase of Godfather Pizza, where he is now CEO. In 1994, Cain was elected president of the National Restaurant Association. He is also a supporter of the Edmonson Foundation Youth Outreach Program for troubled teens.

Alexa Canady (71) became the first African American female neurosurgeon when she was twenty-six years old. She is a certified specialist in pediatric neurosurgery and has taught at the University of Pennsylvania, Henry Ford Hospital, and Wayne State University.

Jack Canfield (14) is co-author (with Mark Victor Hansen) of *Dare to Win* and *Chicken Soup for the Soul,* which sold 1.7 million copies in its first eighteen months and is the first title in a series that continues to have a very long run on the paperback best-seller list.

Emily Card (77) is best known for initiating work, as a Senate fellow, to obtain equal credit for women. The Equal Credit Opportunity Act of 1973 is the result of her efforts. She is also the author of *Business Capital for Women: An Essential Handbook for Entrepreneurs.*

Andrew Carnegie (100, 139), 1835–1919, a Scottish immigrant, entered the iron and steel business and became the chief owner of Homestead Steel Works and seven other steel manufacturers, which he consolidated into the Carnegie Steel Company, and which later merged with United States Steel. He retired in 1901 and spent the rest of his life involved in philanthropy.

Benjamin S. Carson, Sr. (53, 81, 89), after following his mother's advice to read two books a week, went from being the "dumbest kid in the class" to being at the top of his class in one year. Now he is the director of pediatric neurosurgery at Johns Hopkins Hospital in Baltimore, Maryland. With Cecil Murphey, Carson authored two books: *Gifted Hands* and *Think Big: Unleashing Your Potential for Excellence.*

James Earl ("Jimmy") Carter, Jr. (142), is a successful peanut farmer, businessperson, and politician. Carter served in the Georgia State Senate, as governor of Georgia, and as president of the United States from 1977 to 1981. He is currently a volunteer with Habitat for Humanity.

George Washington Carver (35, 48, 79, 89), 1864–1943, the "Wizard of Tuskegee" was the director of agricultural research at Tuskegee Institute in Alabama. His discoveries transformed the agrarian industry of the South. Carver was born into slavery but went on to earn an M.S. degree in agriculture at Iowa Agricultural College.

Catalyst **(76)** is the leading nonprofit organization focusing the attention of business leaders and public policy makers on women's workplace issues.

Emma Chappell (71) is the founder and CEO of the United Bank of Philadelphia.

Clark Childers (32) is the founder (at age seventeen) and president of QuikSkins Boat Covers in Corpus Christi, Texas. Childers' sales for 1994 were $45,000, with profits of $20,000.

Faith Childs (56) is a successful self-employed literary agent.

Shirley Chisholm (16, 84) is the founder and chair of the National Political Congress of Black Women. In 1968 she was the first African American woman to be elected to the U.S. Congress, where she served until 1982. She also ran for President of the United States in 1972 and is the author of *Unbought and Unbossed.*

Deepak Chopra (91, 92) has written sixteen books, including *The Seven Spiritual Laws of Success, Ageless Body, Timeless Mind,* and *The Path to Love,* which have been translated into twenty-five languages. He is also director for educational programs at the Chopra Center for Well Being in La Jolla, California.

Chin-Ning Chu (4, 15, 113) is the president of Asian Marketing Consultants and author of *The Asian Mind Game* and *Thick Face, Black Heart.*

Janean Chun (76, 77) is a senior editor for *Entrepreneur,* a magazine for small businesses.

Winston Churchill (111, 141), 1874–1965, was the Prime Minister of England, 1940–1945 and 1951–1955. He also authored several books, including *My African Journey, Liberalism and the Social Problem, The Unrelenting Struggle,* and a six-volume study, *The Second World War.* He was awarded the Nobel Prize for Literature in 1953.

Jennifer Clark (123) is a partner (with Renee Paige) in the direct-mail-order business A Letter From Home Cookie Company.

Jill Nadine Clements (138) is the owner of Nadina's Cremes, all-natural body creams. She started the business in 1990 and has revenues of about $1 million.

Johnnie Cochran (52, 56, 81) is the cofounder of the law firm Cochran, Mitchell & Lotkin, with offices in Los Angeles and Washington, D.C. In 1991, he was named Trial Lawyer of the Year by the Los Angeles Trial Lawyers Association's board of governors, and he has received the Medgar Evers Award from the National Association for the Advancement of Colored People (NAACP). Cochran's client list has included Geronimo Pratt, O. J. Simpson, Michael Jackson, and victims of the Oklahoma City bombing of a federal building. He authored *Journey to Justice.*

Carol Columbus-Green (7) is president and CEO of Laracris, the nation's only African American female–owned shapewear manufacturer. She has a staff of ten and sales of about $4 million.

Confucius (85, 142) (K'ung Fu-tzu), 551–479 B.C., was a student of ancient literature who gained a reputation for scholarship. He was prime minister of Lu in China then became a traveling teacher, sharing his moral precepts for daily life.

Marlene Connor (9) is a successful self-employed literary agent.

John Calvin Coolidge (115), 1872–1933, was president of the United States from 1925 to 1929.

Don Cornwell (135) is the founder and CEO of Granite Broadcasting, the 1995 *Black Enterprise* Company of the Year. Granite owns nine television stations and had gross revenues of more than $76 million in 1994, up from $45 million in 1993.

William H. ("Bill") Cosby (46, 79, 94) has had several top-rated television shows, including *The Cosby Show, Fat Albert and the Cosby Kids,* and *I Spy.* He is also a successful comedian and commercial spokesperson for a variety of products, and is well-known for his generous philanthropy. Cosby is the author of *Fatherhood, Time Flies,* and *The Wit and Wisdom of Fat Albert.*

Stephen R. Covey (43, 56, 58, 98, 104) is the founder and chair of the Covey Leadership Center and author of *First Things First* and *The Seven Habits of Highly Effective People.*

Mary J. Cronin (98) is the author of *Doing Business on the Internet.*

Theodore L. Cross (129) is the author of *Black Capitalism.*

D

Ronald E. Damper (26) is the founder of the Damron Corporation, suppliers of tea for McDonald's restaurants.

Norma Jean Darden (102) (with her sister Carole) owns Spoonbread, Inc., a catering service in New York with revenues in the six figures. The company's client list includes Bill Cosby and former New York mayor David Dinkins. The sisters are also the authors of *Spoonbread and Strawberry Wine.*

Dale Dauten (35, 142) is the author of the syndicated business column "Corporate Curmudgeon."

Joe Davidson (61) is a contributing editor to *Emerge* and a reporter for *The Wall Street Journal.*

Miles Davis (32, 51, 87, 112, 132) 1926–1991, was a musical innovator and trumpet player extraordinaire. He won several Grammys for *We Want Miles* in 1983 and *Tutu* in 1987. He

was also named Jazz Musician of the Year by *Jazz Forum.*
With Quincy Troupe, he authored *Miles: The Autobiography.*

Ossie Davis (106) is the author and director of the play *Purlie
Victorious,* coproducer (with his wife Ruby Dee) of *Countdown at Kusini,* and an actor who has numerous credits for
performances on stage, screen, and television. He was nominated for an Emmy for his role as Martin Luther King, Sr., in
the television movie *King.*

Patty DeDominic (76) is the founder of PDQ Personnel Services, Inc., in Los Angeles.

Ruby Dee (4, 34, 84) is the author and director of the play
Take It from the Top, coproducer (with her husband Ossie
Davis) of *Countdown at Kusini,* and an actress who has numerous credits for performances on stage, screen, and television. She won an ACE Award for her work in *Long Day's Journey into Night.*

Martin R. Delany (61), 1812–1885, was cofounder and coed-
itor of *The North Star,* a newspaper devoted to the abolition
of slavery. Delany was also an agent for the Underground Railroad and a physician, and he was commissioned as a major
during the Civil War.

W. Edwards Deming (53, 122) is a business consultant whose
consultations with Japanese industry led to new standards of
quality and productivity. He is also author of *Out of the Crisis*
and many other books.

Derrick Dingle (57) is founder (with Dwayne McDuffie,
Denys Cowan, and Michael Davis) of Milestone Media, Inc., a
comic book publisher.

Walter E. ("Walt") Disney (88), 1901–1966, created Donald
Duck, Mickey Mouse, and the full-length animated films *Snow
White and the Seven Dwarfs, Fantasia, Pinocchio,* and others;
and he founded the Disney empire of theme parks, movies,
animation, and television.

Martha Dixon (111) is the owner of Martha's Designs, high-
fashion apparel, in Arkadelphia, Arkansas. Dixon has designed clothes for Hillary Clinton.

Frederick Douglass (29, 49), 1817–1895, was enslaved until
age nineteen years but went on to cofound and coedit *The*

North Star, a newspaper devoted to the abolition of slavery. Douglass was a well-known abolitionist and orator. He authored three autobiographies, including *Life and Times of Frederick Douglass,* and was an advisor to President Abraham Lincoln and Consul to Haiti.

Sunny Drewel (10) is the founder of the mail-order catalog business Linen & Lace, which has annual sales of over $1 million.

Bryan Drysdale (57, 58) is co-author (with Julie Blau) of *Problem Solving for Entrepreneurs: A Creative New Approach to Overcoming Your Business Problems.*

William Edward Burghardt (W. E. B.) DuBois (3, 71), 1868–1963, was a founder of the NAACP, a professor of history and sociology, and the author of more than thirty books, including *The Negro in Business, The Souls of Black Folk, The Suppression of the African Slave Trade,* and *The Philadelphia Negro.*

Karen I. Duckett (22) is the president and CEO of Duckett & Associates, interior designers in Atlanta, Georgia. Duckett's firm has helped to design office complexes, hospitals, and schools. Her team includes architects, urban planners, and interior designers.

Anthony Drexel Duke (139) is the founder of Boys Harbor in North Carolina. He is an heir of the Dukes, who made their money in tobacco and contributed to Trinity College, which became Duke University.

Bill Duke (65) was named Best Young Director at a Houston Film Festival. Duke has performed in a number of films, including *Car Wash, America Gigolo, Action Jackson,* and *Bird on a Wire.* His directing credits include *A Rage in Harlem, Deep Cover,* and *Sister Act 2: Back in the Habit.*

Joe Dumars (110), an All-Star player in the NBA, was the Most Valuable Player in the 1989 championship game and a member of two Detroit Pistons championship teams.

Alexandre Dumas, *fils* **(80),** 1824–1895, was a popular and successful French poet, novelist, and playwright, whose works include *The Lady of the Camelias, Tristam le Roux,* and *The Women's Friend.*

Alexandre Dumas, *pere* **(51, 92),** 1802–1870, was a popular and successful French novelist and playwright, whose works include *The Three Musketeers, The Man in the Iron Mask,* and *Richard Darlington.*

Henry L. Dumas (69), 1934–1968, was a gifted writer whose works were edited by Eugene Redmond and published posthumously. Dumas's books include *Play Ebony, Play Ivory* (originally titled *Poetry for My People); Ark of Bones and Other Stories;* and *Jonah and the Green Stone.*

Faye Dunaway (76), who has her own production company, has appeared in more than forty films. She was nominated for Academy Awards for *Bonnie and Clyde* and *Chinatown,* and she won the best actress Oscar for *Network.*

Paul Laurence Dunbar (37, 134), 1872–1906, was best known for his dialect poetry, but he also published poetry in standard English, as well as several books of fiction. Some of his titles are *Oak and Ivy, Majors and Minors, Lyrics of Lowly Life, The Uncalled,* and *Folks from Dixie.* He also collaborated on an operetta, *Dream Lovers,* with the British musician Samuel Coleridge-Taylor.

Katherine Dunham (58), is the director of the Katherine Dunham Center for the Performing Arts at Southern Illinois University. In the 1930s, she brought major innovations to modern dance by adding elements of African and Caribbean folk dance. Dunham received the Kennedy Center Honors in 1983 and the Scripps American Dance Festival Award in 1986.

Ed Dwight (45), a very successful bronze sculptor in Denver, has done commissioned works for Motown Records, the Atlanta-Fulton County Stadium, and a monument to the Underground Railroad located in Battle Creek, Michigan. Dwight is creating a memorial to the African Americans who fought in the Revolutionary War, to be installed between the Washington and Lincoln memorials in Washington, D.C.

Wayne Dyer (6, 39) is a psychologist, popular motivational speaker, and author of several books, including *Pulling Your Own Strings, Eykis, The Sky's the Limit,* and *Your Erroneous Zones,* which have sold more than 30 million copies around the world.

E

Clint Eastwood (42, 98), who has been a movie and television performer since 1955, formed Malpaso Productions in 1969. He produced, directed, and starred in the film *Unforgiven,* which won Academy Awards for best picture and best director. He also directed and starred in *The Bridges of Madison County.*

Evelyn Echols (125) started the Echols Travel and Hotel Institute in Chicago in 1962 and is still its CEO, at more than eighty years of age. The $1.5 million company trains workers for the travel industry.

Marian Wright Edelman (23, 80, 84, 140) is the founder and president of the Children's Defense Fund, a Washington, D.C., group that lobbies for health, welfare, and justice for children and their families. In 1985, she was awarded a MacArthur Fellowship. She also authored *The Measure of Our Success* and *Guide My Feet.*

Kenneth ("Babyface") Edmonds (133) is a dominant force in popular music. He has written, produced, or performed 111 top-ten popular songs, including 16 number-one singles, and has produced sales of 26 million singles and 72 million albums. Once, he had 12 songs on the Billboard popular (pop) and rhythm-and-blues (R&B) charts at the same time.

Audrey Edwards (43, 61, 66, 134), an editor-at-large for *Essence* magazine, often writes on financial matters. She also writes for other national publications, including *Working Woman* and the *New York Times.* Edwards is co-author (with Craig K. Polite) of *Children of the Dream.*

Michael D. Eisner (100) has been the chair and CEO of Disney Productions and the president and chief operations officer (COO) of Paramount Pictures. He began his career with the programming department at CBS.

Edward Kennedy ("Duke") Ellington (57), 1899–1974, was a legendary jazz musician, composer, and bandleader. He wrote more than 5,000 pieces of music; a few of the best-known are "Mood Indigo," "I Got It Bad and That Ain't Good," and "Don't Get Around Much Anymore." Ellington was the recipient of numerous awards, including Grammys and the Spingarn Medal.

Ralph W. Ellison (106), 1914–1994, wrote *Invisible Man,* which was published in 1952 and won the National Book Award and the National Newspaper Publishers' Russwurm Award. The novel is a classic that has never been out of print. *Invisible Man* was also selected as the most distinguished postwar American novel, and Ellison was chosen as the sixth most influential novelist by a *New York Herald Tribune* poll of writers, editors, and critics.

Ralph Waldo Emerson (39, 59), 1803–1882, was a philosopher, poet, and licensed minister of the Unitarian Church. Emerson lectured, preached, and wrote essays espousing his transcendental philosophy. He is the author of "Self Reliance," *Society and Solitude, Natural History of Intellect, Nature,* and other works.

Ethiopian proverb (106, 109) Ethiopia is a country in northeast Africa.

Mari Evans (54) is a prolific writer of poetry, children's books, drama, and musicals. Her popular book of poetry *I Am a Black Woman* received the first annual poetry award of the Black Academy of Arts and Letters. Evans's books also include *Where is All the Music? Night Star, Jim Flying High, Singing Black,* and *A Dark and Splendid Mass.*

F

Louis Farrakhan (28) (né Louis Walcott) joined the Nation of Islam in 1955 and rose to become the leader of that organization in 1975. The focus of the Nation of Islam is entrepreneurship and self-reliance. In 1995, about a million African American men responded to Farrakhan's call for a day of atonement in Washington, D.C.

Charles F. Feeney (141) is a trustee of the Atlantic Foundation and Atlantic Trust and was a partner in Duty Free Shoppers. In 1984, Feeney turned over his share of Duty Free Shoppers,

Ltd., to his charitable foundation, a gift worth about $500 million at the time, which has grown to about $3.5 billion.

Marsha Feltingoff (118) owns Alma International, Inc., a $20 million company in Boca Raton, Florida.

Aaron Feuerstein (127), the CEO of Malden Mills in Lawrence, Massachusetts, kept most of his workers on the payroll for ninety days, even though his mill had partially burned down. Malden Mills has stayed competitive while remaining located in the United States by creating new textiles such as Polartec, a polyester with the properties of wool.

Malcolm Stevenson Forbes (79), 1919–1990, was chair and editor-in-chief of *Forbes,* a business magazine, from 1954 to 1990. The publication has a circulation of more than 735,000.

Leon Forrest (45), a professor of creative writing and African American Studies at Northwestern University in Evanston, Illinois, authored *The Bloodworth Orphans, There Is a Tree More Ancient Than Eden, Divine Days, Relocations of the Spirit,* and other books.

Alvin Foster (22, 41, 112) is the owner of AMF Mail Advertising, a successful direct-mail and marketing service in Boston, Massachusetts.

John Hope Franklin (29), a leading American historian, is the James B. Duke professor of history at Duke University. He is the author of *From Slavery to Freedom,* first published in 1947 and now in its seventh edition. He has also written *Racial Equality in America, Reconstruction after the Civil War,* and *George Washington Williams: A Biography.*

George Fraser (2, 18, 67, 104, 105, 107, 121, 138) is founder and president of SuccessSource, Inc., based in Cleveland, and publisher of the best-selling *SuccessGuide: The Networking Guide to Black Resources.* He also authored the best-selling book *Success Runs in Our Race.*

Kevin Freiberg and **Jackie Freiberg (137, 142)** are the principals of the San Diego Consulting Group, "equipping leaders for a world of change," and co-authors of *Nuts! Southwest Airlines' Crazy Recipe for Business and Personal Success.*

S. B. Fuller (8, 54), 1905–1988, with only six years of education, was a pioneer in door-to-door sales with the Fuller Products Company, which he started in 1935. He built a conglomerate of companies with sales of more than $10 million a year and with offices in thirty-eight states.

G

Patrice Gaines (37, 81) overcame a number of personal difficulties to become a reporter for the *Washington Post*. She is also the author of *Laughing in the Dark*.

Bundy Gambrell (62) is a Los Angeles real-estate developer.

Mohandas ("Mahatma") Gandhi (21, 39, 46), 1869–1948, was a lawyer, an Indian nationalist and spiritual leader, and the creator of passive resistance.

Edward G. Gardner (33, 59, 112, 142) is the founder and cochair of the board of Soft Sheen hair-care products in Chicago.

Kevin Garnett (132) went directly to the NBA from high school. In his second year as a player for the Minnesota Timberwolves, he was named to the NBA All-Star team.

Marcus Garvey (97), 1887–1940, founded the Universal Negro Improvement Association (UNIA) in 1911 in Jamaica then opened a branch in Harlem in 1916. Garvey was adamant about African Americans owning their own businesses, and he recruited thousands into the UNIA. He also published the *Negro World* newspaper and started the Black Star Line, a steamship company.

Arthur George (A. G.) Gaston (21) was named *Black Enterprise* Entrepreneur of the Century and with good reason. Gaston started the Booker T. Washington Insurance Company in 1932 and in 1987 sold the company to its employees for $3.5 million, less than 10 percent of its value at the time. This industrious Birmingham entrepreneur has also founded or cofounded a number of other businesses, including the Citizens Federal Savings Bank, A.G. Gaston Construction, Smith & Gaston Funeral Directors, and BTW Broadcasting Service. Gaston's companies had more than $24 million in revenues in 1991. Gaston's autobiography, published in 1968, was entitled *Green Power.*

Henry Louis Gates, Jr. (106), the chair of African American Studies at Harvard University, has edited and authored a number of books, including *The Signifying Monkey: Towards a Theory of Afro-American Literary Criticism,* and *Colored People.* He received the MacArthur Prize in 1981 and has also received grants from the Ford and Rockefeller foundations and the National Endowment for the Humanities.

William ("Bill") Gates (18, 124, 127) is the chair of Microsoft, the world's leading developer of software for personal computers. The company is valued on the stock market at $75 billion.

Carole J. Gellineau (105) owns Carole Joy Creations, Inc., the country's largest African American–owned greeting card business, with sales of more than $2 million. Gellineau has received the Louie Award from the Greeting Card Association; the award is given annually to the company that exhibits creative excellence in the industry.

Gikuyu proverb (97) The Gikuyu are a people who reside primarily in Kenya.

Nikki Giovanni (81), a professor in the English department at Virginia Polytechnic Institute and State University in Blacksburg, is best known as a poet and author of several books, including *The Selected Poems of Nikki Giovanni, Black Feeling, Black Talk, Spin a Soft Black Song: Poems for Black Children, Gemini,* and *Racism 101,* as well as the recording *Truth Is on Its Way.* Giovanni has received honorary degrees and numerous awards, including the *Mademoiselle* award for outstanding achievement and the National Association of Radio and Television Announcers award for best spoken-word album.

Raymond Gleason (35) is a professor of strategy and creativity at George Fox University in Newberg, Oregon.

Jere W. Glover (11, 13) is the chief counsel of the Small Business Administration's Office of Advocacy.

Whoopi Goldberg (94) (née Caryn Johnson) is a comedienne and actress who has starred in thirty movies since 1985, when she appeared in her first movie, *The Color Purple,* for which she received an Academy Award nomination. In 1990, she won an Oscar for her role in *Ghosts,* and she has hosted the Academy Awards ceremony twice. Goldberg has also received the NAACP Image Award and been an *Essence* magazine Woman of the Year.

Ross E. Goldstein (118) is president of Generation Insights, a San Francisco–based firm that tracks trends in the marketplace.

Daisy Gonwe (20) is one of hundreds of "doily mamas," entrepreneurs in Zimbabwe who knit scraps of cloth into useful items, which they sell in more affluent South Africa.

Phil Goodman (119) is the founder of the Boomer Marketing & Research Center in San Diego and author of *The Boomer Marketing Revolution*.

Paul Goodnight (10, 112) is a successful Boston artist whose paintings have been featured on television shows such as *The Fresh Prince of Bel-Air*.

Berry Gordy (7, 57, 98, 120) is the founder and former board chair of Motown Industries, which produced a number of popular recording artists, including Diana Ross and the Supremes, Smokey Robinson and the Miracles, Marvin Gaye, Martha and the Vandellas, and Stevie Wonder. Among the movies Gordy produced are *Lady Sings the Blues* and *Bingo Long and His Traveling All-Stars*. He was inducted into the Rock and Roll Hall of Fame in 1988 and is the author of *To Be Loved: The Music, the Magic, the Memories of Motown*.

Milton Gralla (43, 125, 141) and his brother Larry are former owners of Gralla Publications, a business that started a number of trade magazines. They sold the company in 1983 for $73 million. Milton is co-author (with Adriane Berg) of *How Good Guys Grow Rich*.

Denyce Graves (23) is an international opera star with bookings into the next century. Many critics call her *Carmen* performance the definitive one. She made her debut at the New York Metropolitan Opera in the role.

Earl G. Graves (8, 13, 29), author of *How to Succeed in Business Without Being White,* is the founder of *Black Enterprise* magazine and CEO of Earl G. Graves Enterprises, Ltd. The magazine encourages and supports African American business aspirations and has a circulation of approximately 350,000.

Flora Green (17), the founder of Foliage by Flora, Inc., in Miami, is the winner (with her partner Jo Gillman) of the 1996 Entrepreneurial Woman Small-Business Owner of the Year.

Shelley Green (129) is co-author (with Paul Pryde) of *Black Entrepreneurship in America*.

Jill Griffin (123, 124) is the president of The Marketing Resource Center, Inc., a strategic marketing company in Austin, Texas, and the author of *Customer Loyalty: How to Earn It, How to Keep It.*

Mark Griffin (135) is Utah's security administrator.

Florence ("Flo-Jo") Griffith-Joyner (80) writes a fitness column for *USA Weekend* and has designed sports apparel, but she is best known as a track star. Griffith-Joyner set gold-medal records in the women's 100-meter and 200-meter races at the 1988 Olympic games.

David Guidry (57) is the president of Guico Machine Works, Inc., a machine parts manufacturer in Harvey, Louisiana.

Lani Guinier (64) is a professor of law at the University of Pennsylvania and author of *The Tyranny of the Majority.* She came to public attention when she refused to go away quietly when President Clinton withdrew her nomination for assistant attorney general for civil rights in the U.S. Department of Justice.

H

Sharon Hadary (71) is executive director of the National Foundation of Women Business Owners, Silver Spring, Maryland.

Richard Hagberg (11, 96) is president of Hagberg Consulting Group in Foster City, California. The firm did a study of the traits that set entrepreneurs apart from corporate executives.

Birdie M. Hale (16), an eighty-year-old actress, has been seen in a number of movies, commercials, and sitcoms.

Lorraine Hansberry (12, 132), 1930–1965, was a playwright who wrote the acclaimed play *Raisin in the Sun,* which won the New York Drama Critics Circle Award. She also wrote *The Sign in Sidney Brustein's Window* and *Les Blancs.*

Mark Victor Hansen (111, 117) is co-author (with Jack Canfield) of *Dare to Win* and *Chicken Soup for the Soul,* which sold 1.7 million copies in its first eighteen months and is the first title in a series that continues to have a very long run on the paperback best-seller list.

Andre Harrell (53, 141) is the president and CEO of Motown Records.

Bernard Harris (109), is a physician and a National Aeronautics and Space Administration (NASA) astronaut.

Fran Harris (6, 13, 93, 97) authored *About My Sister's Business: The Black Woman's Road Map to Successful Entrepreneurship.*

Lois Harry (72, 75) authored *Stressors, Beliefs and Coping Behaviors of Black Women Entrepreneurs.*

Christopher Hegarty (103) is a management consultant in Novato, California.

Dorothy I. Height (66) is the president of the National Council of Negro Women.

Grant Hill (125) is a professional basketball player for the Detroit Pistons and a three-time NBA All-Star player.

Jesse Hill, Jr. (103, 107), is the retired chair of Atlanta Life Insurance Company and one of the first African American actuaries. He is a former president of the Atlanta Chamber of Commerce and a partner in Concessions International, a vendor of food and beverages for airports.

Napoleon Hill (43, 44, 46, 49, 54, 60, 129), 1883–1970, was a scholar of the science of human success, and author of *Think and Grow Rich* and *You Can Work Your Own Miracles,* and co-author (with Dennis Kimbro) of *Think and Grow Rich: A Black Choice.*

Amy Hilliard-Jones (119) is the founder of Hilliard-Jones Marketing Group, based in Chicago. The company specializes in marketing to ethnic niches.

Ernest Holsendolph (74) writes the column "Minding Our Business" in *Emerge: America's Black Newsmagazine* and is a business columnist for *The Atlanta Journal-Constitution.*

Evander Holyfield (19) won the world heavyweight boxing championship in 1996, beating Mike Tyson when few expected him to do so. Holyfield has won thirty-four of thirty-six bouts.

Tom Hopkins (121) is a sales trainer and the author of *How to Master the Art of Selling.*

Michele Hoskins (7, 95) is the founder and owner of Michele Foods, a multimillion-dollar business in LaGrange, Illinois, which specializes in pancake syrups.

Warrington Hudlin (1, 63) (with his brother Reginald) produced the movies *House Party, House Party 2,* and *Boomerang.* He is also president of the Black Filmmaker Foundation.

Wade Hudson (95) is owner (with his wife Cheryl) of Just Us Books, publishers of books featuring African American children and young people. The company was started in 1988 in East Orange, New Jersey, and has more than 3 million books in print and annual revenues of $1.5 million.

Langston Hughes (16), 1902–1967, was possibly the best-known and most prolific African American writer. He published in nearly every genre: poetry, drama, fiction, essay, biography, and history. Some of his books are *Simple Speaks His Mind, The Ways of White Folks, The Weary Blues, The Panther and the Lash, Fight for Freedom: The Story of the NAACP,* and *The Book of Negro Folklore.* He also won a number of awards and grants.

Bobbi Humphrey (34, 74) is a jazz flutist who established her own record label, Paradise Sounds, and has her own production company, Bobbi Humphrey Music.

Aldous Huxley (82), 1894–1963, was the author of several novels and essays, including *Point Counter Point, Brief Candles, Brave New World,* and *After Many a Summer Dies the Swan.*

I

Iman (Abdulmajid) (79) launched her own eponymous line of cosmetics in 200 JCPenney stores in 1994. She is also an internationally known fashion model and actress.

Robert Imbriale (34, 101) is president of Classique, Inc., a marketing consulting firm in Commack, New York.

Paula Inniss (8) is the owner of Ohio Full Court Press, a digital printing company, and winner of the 1996 Entrepreneurial Woman Start-Up Business of the Year.

Allen Iverson (17), a professional basketball player for the Philadelphia 76ers, was the 1996 number one draft choice of the NBA and was also named Rookie of the Year.

J

Harold Jackson (119) owns Jackson Heath Public Relations International, based in Atlanta.

Jesse L. Jackson (7, 15), who has promoted economic advancement for African Americans for more than twenty-five years, founded Operation PUSH and the Rainbow Coalition. The two organizations have merged into the Rainbow PUSH Action Network, with offices in Chicago and Washington, D.C. Jackson was a candidate for president of the United States in 1984 and 1988.

Leon Jackson (12) founded Multi-Fac Corporation, a bakery licensed to provide products for the Sara Lee Corporation. He is also president of Bill's Shades and Blind Service, Inc., in Chicago.

Phil Jackson (52, 79, 81, 109) is the head coach of the five-time NBA champion Chicago Bulls professional basketball team. He was named Coach of the Year in 1996 and is the author of *Sacred Hoops: Spiritual Lessons of a Hardwood Warrior.*

Reginald ("Reggie") Martinez Jackson (80) was such a successful home-run hitter in the World Series that he was nicknamed "Mr. October," and broke Babe Ruth's record for the highest number of hits in World Series competition. Jackson began playing major league baseball in 1967.

Mae Jemison (48) is director of The Jemison Institute for Advancing Technology in Developing Countries and runs The Jemison Group, Inc., a technology institute working on a satellite-based telecommunication system to improve health care in West Africa. She is also a professor in Dartmouth College's Environmental Studies program. In 1992, she was the first African American female NASA astronaut.

Earvin ("Magic") Johnson (66, 85, 101) opened a very profitable movie multiplex in South Central Los Angeles and plans to open others in central cities around the country. He also owns a sports apparel business. Johnson won five NBA championships with the Los Angeles Lakers and was named one of the fifty greatest players in the history of the NBA.

John H. Johnson (15, 44, 66, 85, 95, 102, 133) succeeded against the odds to become a multimillionaire as the founder and CEO of Johnson Publishing Company, publishers of the popular *Ebony* (circulation close to 2 million) and *Jet* (circulation nearly 1 million) magazines.

Michael Johnson (18, 38, 80, 85), in 1996, became the first athlete ever to win gold medals in both the 200-meter and the 400-meter races in the same Olympic games. He is the author of *Slaying the Dragon: How to Turn Your Small Steps to Great Feats.*

Robert L. Johnson (68) is the founder, chair, and CEO of BET Holdings, Inc., which is traded on the New York Stock Exchange, and owns Black Entertainment Television, a cable network; *Emerge,* a black newsmagazine; BET on Jazz; and BET Movies/Starz!3.

Robert L. ("Bob") Johnson (50, 129) is the founder (with his daughter Rhonda) of Johnson Bryce, a Memphis company that prints and laminates large rolls of thermoplastic film used to make packaging. The business employs fifty people and has revenues of more than $20 million.

Ronald Johnson (65) is the executive director of the National Family Life Center in Los Angeles.

James Earl Jones (67) has a distinctive voice, often heard in commercials and in voice roles such as Darth Vader in the *Star Wars* movies and King Mufasa in *The Lion King.* He received a Medal for Spoken Language from the American Academy of Arts and Letters. Jones is a busy actor, working steadily in theater, film, and television. He has been awarded both a Tony and an Emmy.

Quincy Jones (51, 108, 123) owns QWest Records, a company that has produced music albums for Michael Jackson, Brandy, Ray Charles, Gloria Estefan, Herbie Hancock, and many others. He has also produced and scored movies (such as *The Color Purple, The Pawnbroker, Cactus Flower,* and *The Wiz*) and television shows (*The Fresh Prince of Bel-Air* and *Roots,* for which he won an Emmy) and has won more than two dozen Grammys. He also produced the 1996 Academy Awards show.

Barbara Jordan (54), 1936–1996, came to national attention in 1974 with her eloquent and judicious performance as a member of the U.S. Congressional committee investigating White House misconduct in the "Watergate" hearings. She was a representative from Texas to the U.S. Congress from 1972 to 1978 and then a professor of political values and ethics at the University of Texas until her death.

June Jordan (6, 94) is a poet, novelist, and essayist. She has received a Rockefeller grant for creative writing, and her book *The Voice of the Children* was a *New York Times* selection as one of 1971's outstanding young-adult novels. She has also received fellowships from Yaddo and the National Endowment for the Arts. Her published books include *Who Look at Me, Some Changes, His Own Where,* and *On Call: New Political Essays.*

Michael Jordan (24, 32, 83, 99) has held the NBA scoring title a record nine times and was named Most Valuable Player of the five Chicago Bulls championship teams. He has been named to the All-Star team each year he has played professional basketball and is one of the fifty greatest players in the history of the NBA.

Jackie Joyner-Kersee (24) was called the world's greatest female athlete when she set a gold medal record in the Heptathlon at the 1988 Olympic games. She also won the gold in the long jump at the 1988 Olympics. Joyner-Kersee won the Heptathlon again in 1992 and a bronze medal in the long jump in 1996. She is currently playing professional basketball in the American Basketball Leauge (ABL).

K

John Kao (31, 37) has founded companies in biotechnology, feature films, and video computing; has taught at Harvard and Stanford university business schools; and authored *Jamming.*

June Kelly (45) is an art dealer and owner of the June Kelly Gallery in New York City.

Danielle Kennedy (29, 83, 101, 111, 122, 126) is the author of *Selling—The Danielle Kennedy Way* and a contributing writer to *Entrepreneur*, a magazine for small businesses.

Florynce ("Flo") Kennedy (4), an attorney and outspoken social activist, is the co-author of *Abortion Rap*.

Lamont Kennerly (136) is owner (with his partner Frank Conwell) of Soft & Precious hair and skin products, specially formulated for African American babies. The products are sold by such chains as Wal-Mart, Winn Dixie, and Eckerd, with sales expected to reach $500,000 in 1997.

Geoffrey Kessler (127) is president of the Kessler Exchange, a small-business research firm in Northridge, California.

Dennis Kimbro (43, 44, 46, 60, 67, 107, 129) is director of the Clark Atlanta University Center for Entrepreneurship and author of *What Makes the Great Great: Strategies for Extraordinary Achievement*. Kimbro is also the author of two best-selling books, *Think and Grow Rich: A Black Choice* (with Napoleon Hill) and *Daily Motivations for African American Success*.

Riley ("B.B.") King (23), the legendary blues singer and innovative guitarist, received the Kennedy Center Honors in 1995. King has a Blues Club and Restaurant in Los Angeles and has written his autobiography, *Blues All around Me*.

Elizabeth King (49) owns King Management Consulting and administers the Entrepreneurship Training Program for the Women's Self-Employment Project in Chicago.

Hazel A. King (10) owns H.A. King Associates, a marketing and communications consulting company in Chicago. King has been recognized for her work to promote business development and education among minorities and women by the Women's Business Development Center of the U.S. Small Business Administration and *Inc.* magazine.

Martin Luther King, Jr. (56, 58, 59), 1929–1968, led the nonviolent passive-resistance civil-rights movement and was awarded the 1964 Nobel Prize for Peace. King also authored several books, including *Stride Toward Freedom: The Montgomery Story, The Measure of a Man, Why We Can't Wait,* and *The Trumpet of Conscience.*

Eartha Kitt (84) began her career as a dancer with Katherine Dunham and was a singer and had her own club in Paris. She also toured Europe with Orson Welles's stage production of *Faust*. She appeared in the movies *Fatal Instinct* and *Boomerang* and on stage in *Timbuktu*.

Gloria Knight (78) is the retired president of Jamaica Mutual Life Assurance Society, Kingston, Jamaica.

Jennifer Kraljevich (126) is president of Tezcatlipoca, Inc., an Internet service provider in Chicago with about 1,500 customers.

Jawanza Kunjufu (65) is the owner of African American Images, a publishing company in Chicago, and the author of a number of books, including *Black Economics: Solutions for Economic and Community Empowerment*.

Sandra L. Kurtzig (15, 55) is the founder and former CEO of ASK Computer Systems.

Jennifer Kushell (30) is president of The Young Entrepreneurs Network. Kushell started four small businesses while a student at Boston University.

L

Patti LaBelle (41, 139) (née Patricia Louise Holt) has earned a number of gold records. In addition to being a very successful and popular singer, she is also an actress, having appeared in movies and on her own television sitcom. She is a philanthropist and author of *Don't Block the Blessings: Revelations of a Lifetime*. She formerly was the lead singer with the group The Bluebelles.

Edwin C. Laird (126) is the founder and president of Coatings Resource Corporation, a specialty manufacturer of paints and coatings in Huntington Beach, California.

Edwin H. Land (34, 56) holds more U.S. patents than any other inventor except Thomas Edison. He invented instant photography and is the founder of the Polaroid Corporation.

Shelton J. ("Spike") Lee (13, 52, 112, 136) is the CEO of Forty Acres and a Mule Filmworks, Inc., of Brooklyn, New

York. Lee wrote, produced, directed, and acted in *School Daze, Do the Right Thing, Mo' Better Blues, Malcolm X,* and a number of other movies. He received the Los Angeles Film Critics Award for Best New Director for *She's Gotta Have It.*

Rieva Lesonsky (25, 136) is editor-in-chief of *Entrepreneur,* a magazine for small businesses.

Steve Leveen (124) (with his wife Lori) created the *Levenger* catalog, offering "tools for serious readers" and generating revenues of $60 million.

Jay Conrad Levinson (113, 116, 117, 118, 120) writes the "Guerrilla Marketing" column for *Entrepreneur,* the magazine for small businesses. He is the author of the *Guerrilla Marketing* series of books and cofounder of Guerrilla Marketing International.

Edward ("Ed") Lewis (21) was a member of the Hollingsworth Group in 1970, which founded *Essence,* a magazine for African American women. Lewis is also the publisher and CEO of *Essence,* which has a circulation well over 1 million.

Frederick Carlton ("Carl") Lewis (93, 131), once the world's fastest runner, won his ninth gold medal in track at age thirty-five, having earned the medals during four successive Olympic games.

John Lewis (40, 53) has been featured in a Humana Health Care television commercial.

Loida Nicolas Lewis (70) is the chair and CEO of TLC Beatrice International Holdings, Inc., a food processor and distributor with a net income of $15 million in 1995.

Margie Lewis (123) is president and CEO of Parallax, Inc., a $13 million engineering and environmental management company with offices in Maryland, Georgia, Tennessee, Texas, and Kentucky.

Michael Lewis (63) is a senior editor for *The New Republic,* a weekly magazine published out of Washington, D.C., which examines contemporary issues.

Reginald F. Lewis (62, 64, 86, 94, 96, 106), 1942–1993, was a lawyer, financier, and philanthropist; at his death, he was CEO and major shareholder of TLC Beatrice International Holdings, Inc., a food processor and distributor.

Terry Lewis (43) (with Jimmy "Jam" Harris) won the 1986 Grammy for Best Producers of the Year. The talented partners have worked with Janet Jackson, Patti Austin, Gladys Knight, and Johnny Gill, among others. In 1992, they formed their own label, Perspective Records.

Rae Lewis-Thornton (59, 73) is a leading and outspoken AIDS activist who travels across the country speaking to schools, churches, colleges, and wherever else she can, to issue a warning to those who believe they are not at risk from AIDS. She graduated college magna cum laude with a degree in political science and worked in both of Jesse Jackson's presidential campaigns and in Carol Moseley-Braun's successful U.S. Senate campaign.

James A. Lindsay (26) is the founder of Rap Snacks Food, a company that distributes unusual potato chip flavors, such as Bar-B-Quing With My Honey and Got That Chili Cheese. In 1994, his first year in business, he grossed $1 million.

James Bruce Llewellyn (15, 20, 45, 95, 105, 127) is the majority partner of Queen City Broadcasting, Inc., a Buffalo, New York, company valued at $110 million. He also co-owns the Philadelphia Coca-Cola Bottling Company, which was number 3 on the 1995 *Black Enterprise* list of the 100 top-grossing African American industrial/service businesses.

Glynn Lloyd (96) is a cofounder and owner (with Jonathan Ruelas and Earl West) of City Fresh Caterers in Roxbury, Massachusetts. They specialize in ethnic foods and have an account with Meals on Wheels, as well as doing special-events catering.

Joe Louis (131) (né Joseph Louis Barrow), 1911–1981, retired as undefeated world heavyweight boxing champion in 1949. He won sixty-eight of seventy-one bouts and entered the Boxing Hall of Fame in 1954.

M

Harvey Mackay (47, 126) is a business consultant and author of *Beware the Naked Man Who Offers You His Shirt* and *Swim with the Sharks without Being Eaten Alive*.

Karl Malone (99) owns a trucking company but is best known as a professional basketball player for the Utah Jazz. He is a perennial All-Star player and was named one of the fifty greatest players in the history of the NBA.

Julianne Malveaux (62) is a nationally known economist, columnist, and television and radio commentator. Her syndicated column appears twice weekly in newspapers across the country. Malveaux is vice president of the National Association of Negro Business and Professional Women's Clubs and the author of *Sex, Lies and Stereotypes: Perspectives of a Mad Economist.*

Tony March (137) is a General Motors dealer in Hartford, Connecticut.

Alfred Marcus (9) is a professor of strategic management at the University of Minnesota in Minneapolis and author of *Business and Society: Strategy Ethics in the Global Economy.*

Marilyn Marcus (3) is a family counselor in Chicago.

Marjorie Margolies-Mezvinsky (56) is a former member of the U.S. House of Representatives from Pennsylvania.

John Tepper Marlin (137) is an economist and social auditor in New York City.

Curtis Mayfield (10, 87) is a rhythm-and-blues singer and songwriter whose most recent album is *New World Order.* He has produced a number of hit records, including "He Will Break Your Heart," "Hey Little Girl," and "Gypsy Woman." He may be best known for his sound track of the 1970s movie *Superfly.*

Roberta Maynard (101) is associate editor of *Nation's Business,* a magazine for small businesses.

Benjamin E. Mays (42, 113), 1895–1984, was a sharecropper's son who became president of Morehouse College in Atlanta, where he served from 1940 to 1968. In 1970, Mays was the first African American elected president of the board of the Atlanta Public Schools. His autobiography is *Born to Rebel.*

William G. Mays (127) is the founder and president of Mays Chemical Company in Indianapolis.

Clotee McAfee (67) is the founder and owner of Deljah Simone Inc., a Los Angeles clothing manufacturer.

Susan McCann (66) is president of City Lands, the real estate division of Shorebank Corporation, a redevelopment group in Chicago.

Osceola McCarty (20) earned her living washing clothes, then donated her life savings of $150,000 to the University of Southern Mississippi for college scholarships.

David C. McClelland (24) is the author of *The Achieving Society*.

Lee McCord (11, 137) is the owner of McCord & Associates, a polygraph examiner business in Chicago.

Robert ("Bobby") McFerrin, Jr. (24), is most widely known for his vocal albums, *Simple Pleasures* (with the hit song "Don't Worry, Be Happy") and *Medicine Music*. McFerrin is a consummate musician, who also played piano professionally until 1977. In 1989, he began studying conducting and made his debut as a conductor with the San Francisco Symphony in 1990.

Jimmy McJamerson (32) is the owner of JMc-Positive Black Images Inc. and a history professor at Grambling State University in Louisiana.

Jacob R. Miles (27) is the founder (in 1988) and creative force at Cultural Exchange Corporation, a full-line toy company that specializes in ethnic toys, games, puzzles, posters, and greeting cards for special occasions and holidays.

Lorraine Miller (8, 130) owns Cactus & Tropicals, a plant store in Salt Lake City, Utah, with annual sales of $2 million. She was named Small Business Person of the Year in 1994.

Robert Miller (28) is vice president for marketing at the Federal Express Corporation.

James Moore (31, 33, 90, 103, 105, 119, 126) authored *The Death of Competition*.

Akio Morita (40, 43, 117), a founder of the Sony Corporation, authored *Made in Japan,* the story of Sony's origins and subsequent development.

Toni Morrison (5, 32, 39, 50) (née Chloe Anthony Wofford) became the first African American to be awarded the Nobel Prize in Literature in 1993. She has also received the National Book Critics Circle Award for *Song of Solomon* and the

Pulitzer Prize for *Beloved*. Her other books include *The Bluest Eye, Tar Baby, Playing in the Dark,* and *Jazz.*

Walter Mosley (48, 98) has received a Golden Dagger Award in England and been nominated twice for an Edgar Award. His novels have been translated into seventeen languages, and he is a favorite of President Clinton. Mosley is the author of the Easy Rawlins mysteries: *Gone Fishin', Devil in a Blue Dress* (which was made into a movie), *A Red Death, White Butterfly, Black Betty,* and *A Little Yellow Dog.*

Constance Baker Motley (28), in 1966, became the first African American woman to be named to a federal judgeship. Motley worked for 20 years with the NAACP Legal Defense Fund and was the only woman elected to the New York Senate in 1964. She also served four years as chief judge of the southern district of New York.

N

Gloria Naylor (106) received the American Book Award for best first novel for *The Women of Brewster Place* and the Distinguished Writer Award from the Mid-Atlantic Writers Association in 1983. She has been the recipient of a National Endowment for the Arts fellowship and a Candace Award. Naylor's other works include *Linden Hills* and *Mama Day.*

Thomas H. Naylor (14) is a professor at Duke University and co-author (with Rolf Osterberg and William Willimon) of *The Search for Meaning in the Workplace.*

Donn Nettles (98) has a naprapathy and preventive medicine business in Chicago.

David Newton (78) is a professor of business at Westmont College in Santa Barbara, California, and a consultant to small businesses.

Nigerian proverb (50) Nigeria is a country in West Africa.

Jessye Norman (58), an exceptionally gifted soprano, won the Munich Competition in 1968 and made her operatic debut at the Berlin Deutsche Opera in 1969. She sang *Aida* at La Scala in Milan and Cassandre in *Troyens* in London's Covent Garden, the role in which she made her debut at the New York Metropolitan in 1986.

Eleanor Holmes Norton (73) has been a representative in the U.S. Congress from Washington, D.C., since 1991. She is a former chair of the U.S. Equal Employment Opportunity Commission.

Michael Novak (9, 36), a theologian who studied for the Catholic priesthood, has written twenty-five books on philosophy, theology, politics, economics, and culture, including *Business as a Calling: Work and the Examined Life.*

O

Odetta (5) (née Holmes Felious Gordon), an internationally acclaimed songwriter, folksinger, and guitarist, has had singing roles in several films, including *Sanctuary.*

Shaquille O'Neal (27, 130) entered the NBA when he was twenty years old, made his first rap album at age twenty-two, won the NBA scoring title at twenty-three, and starred in his first feature film at twenty-four. He has also been an All-Star player every year and was selected one of the fifty greatest players in the history of the NBA.

Rolf Osterberg (14) is a Swedish businessperson and co-author (with Thomas H. Naylor and William Willimon) of *The Search for Meaning in the Workplace.*

B. Denise Owens (47, 134), the owner of a very successful Allstate agency in Indianapolis, was awarded the insurance industry's National Quality Award in 1991. Owens is a Life Underwriter Training Council Fellow, a fifteen-time winner of the Allstate Honor Ring, and a five-time recipient of the Life Leaders Award.

Michael Owens (78) has been a financial analyst at Eli Lilly Company, in Indianapolis, for twenty-five years. He is the Provincial Keeper of the Exchequer and a member of the Province Board for Kappa Alpha Psi Fraternity. Owens is a volunteer with the Washington Township Schools Parents Advisory Council, the Boy Scouts, and Big Brothers.

P

Clarence Page (27) is a Pulitzer Prize–winning syndicated columnist for the *Chicago Tribune* and the author of *Showing My Color: Impolite Essays on Race and Identity*. Page is also a frequent contributor to PBS's *Newshour* and appears regularly on BET's *Lead Story*.

Heather Page (8) is a staff writer for *Entrepreneur*, a magazine for small businesses.

James Palmer (68) is the owner of Service Livery, the largest taxi service on the south side of Chicago.

Robert Parish (17) played professional basketball in the NBA for twenty-one years, longer than any other player. Parish won NBA championships with the Boston Celtics and the Chicago Bulls and was selected as one of the fifty greatest players in the history of the NBA.

Gordon Parks (51, 101) did not complete high school but has been awarded twenty-eight honorary degrees and the National Medal of Arts from President Reagan in 1988. Parks's magnificent career has included creating photographic essays for *Life* magazine, authoring books *The Learning Tree* and *Arias in Silence*, composing a piano sonata, and making films. He directed and produced *The Learning Tree* and *Shaft*.

Saundra Parks (26) is the founder and president of The Daily Blossom, a floral design company in New York City with revenues of more than $1 million. Parks's clients include HBO, American Express, and Sony Music, as well as Maya Angelou, Spike Lee, and Whitney Houston.

Walter Payton (101) owns restaurants and has other business interests in the Chicago area, but he is best known for his prowess on the football field. Payton led his conference in yards rushed for five seasons, from 1976 to 1980. He also won a Super Bowl championship in 1986 with the Chicago Bears and is a member of the Pro Football Hall of Fame.

Drew Pearson (128) is CEO of Drew Pearson Companies, a sports apparel business located in Addison, Texas.

M. Scott Peck (23, 58) is a psychiatrist and the author of the classic best-seller *The Road Less Traveled*. Peck spends 200 days a year speaking on psychospiritual issues. His other books, *The People of the Lie* and *What Return Can I Make?* are also best-sellers.

Michael Pellecchia (2) is a freelance reviewer and columnist for the *Minneapolis Star Tribune.*

Egbert Perry (107) is a partner in the Integral Group, an urban planning and development group in Atlanta, Georgia.

Robin Petgrave (114) is the owner of Bravo Helicopters, a flight school and tour business in Torrance, California.

Bruce D. Phillips (30) is the director of economic research for the Small Business Administration's Office of Advocacy.

Craig K. Polite (61, 134) is a clinical and industrial psychologist and co-author (with Audrey Edwards) of *Children of the Dream.*

Faith Popcorn (117) owns Brain-Reserve, a marketing consulting firm that pinpoints the forces shaping tomorrow's marketplace. She is the author of *Clicking.*

C. C. H. Pounder (75), a successful actress, has performed in movies including *All That Jazz, Prizzi's Honor, Postcards from the Edge,* and *Sliver.* She has a recurring role in the television series *E.R.*

Alvin Poussaint (104) is a professor of psychiatry at the Harvard University Medical School and was a consultant to *The Cosby Show* television series that ran for eight years.

Adam Clayton Powell, Jr. (39), 1908–1972, was a cleric, a civil-rights leader, and representative to the U.S. Congress from Harlem for eleven consecutive terms.

Colin Powell (8, 98, 99) retired as a four-star general in the U.S. Army, having worked at the Pentagon as national security advisor and chair of the Joint Chiefs of Staff for three U.S. presidents. His best-selling autobiography is *My American Journey.* Powell is the national chair of the volunteer effort America's Promise: The Alliance for Youth.

Leontyne Price (94), a soprano, debuted as a concert singer in New York in 1954. She performed the title role in *Aida* at La Scala in Milan, and she was Leona in *Il Trovatore* at the Metropolitan in New York. She received the Medal of Freedom and the National Medal of the Arts.

The Artist Formerly Known As Prince (10) (né Prince Rogers Nelson) is the owner of Paisley Park Enterprises and a musician, composer, and performer. He has released more than 20 albums and sold in excess of 100 million records around the world.

Lou Pritchett (34, 121) is the retired vice president of sales for Procter & Gamble Company, where he worked for thirty-six years. He is the author of *Stop Paddling and Start Rocking the Boat: Business Lessons from the School of Hard Knocks.*

Ernesta Procope (119) is founder (in 1953), president, and CEO of E.G. Bowman Company, a commercial insurance brokerage firm located on Wall Street in New York City.

Barbara Proctor (22, 74) is the founder (1970) and CEO of Proctor Communications Network, Inc., an advertising agency in Chicago, which has annual billings of about $6 million.

Deborah Prothrow-Stith (100) is the assistant dean of the Harvard School of Public Health. She was formerly the health commissioner for the Commonwealth of Massachusetts and is the author of *Deadly Consequences.*

Paul Pryde (129) is co-author (with Shelley Green) of *Black Entrepreneurship in America.*

R

John Raye (9, 17, 42, 68) is a founder and president of The Majestic Eagles, a Washington, D.C., business development organization that encourages entrepreneurship.

Dary Rees (90) is the owner of Dary Rees Corporation, a home-decor accessories business with revenues of $3.5 million.

Patricia Reid-Merritt (72) is a professor of social work and African American studies at the Richard Stockton College of New Jersey. Reid-Merritt, a well-known community and social activist who speaks before national conferences, authored *Sister Power: How Phenomenal Black Women Are Rising to the Top.*

Rachel Remen (4) is the cofounder and medical director of the Commonweal Cancer Help Program in Bolinas, California, and author of *Kitchen Table Wisdom: Stories That Heal.*

Barbara Reynolds (22) founded Reynolds News Service, a think tank on race, gender, and religion. She was formerly a columnist for *USA Today*.

Jack Ricchiuto (32, 36) is a management consultant and author of *Collaborative Creativity*.

Pat Riley (3, 12, 59, 85, 90, 102, 141) is the head coach and part owner of the Miami Heat professional basketball team. He won four NBA championships as the coach of the Los Angeles Lakers and is the only coach to be named Coach of the Year for three different teams. Riley is the author of *The Winner Within*.

Jack Roosevelt ("Jackie") Robinson (49, 62), 1919–1972, was a businessperson and the first player to break the barrier against African Americans in professional baseball. Robinson was elected to the Baseball Hall of Fame in 1962. He is the author of *I Never Had It Made*.

T. J. Robinson (125) is president and CEO of T.J.'s Gingerbread House in Oakland, California, with annual revenues of $1 million. She is planning to manufacture and package her specialties for sale in grocery stores.

William ("Smokey") Robinson, Jr. (7), is a record producer and record-company executive, as well as a rhythm-and-blues performer. He sang with the Miracles and as a solo act and wrote many hit songs, including "Shop Around," "Tracks of My Tears," and "Tears of a Clown." He also wrote his autobiography, *Inside My Life*.

Dennis Rodman (44, 113) has been on four NBA championship teams, two with the Detroit Pistons and two with the Chicago Bulls. He also led the league in rebounding six years.

John W. Rogers, Jr. (138), is president of Ariel Capital Management Inc., of Chicago, which manages $1.2 billion in assets. Rogers volunteers as president of the Board of the Chicago Park District and heads the Ariel Foundation, which works to develop academic and social potential among economically disadvantaged youths.

Wayne Allyn Root (56, 60, 81, 83, 89, 110, 112), after a long series of disappointments, is now an on-air personality for USA Networks. Root earns between $5,000 and $15,000 for his motivational talks and wrote the book *The Joy of Failure*.

Martha Rothman (124) is the president of Rothman Rothman Heineman Architects in Boston.

William ("Bill") Felton Russell (16, 18, 93) played professional basketball for the Boston Celtics and was the star player of eleven championship teams. Russell also coached in the NBA and was named one of the fifty greatest players in the history of the NBA.

Patricia Russell-McCloud (5) founded and owns Russell-McCloud and Associates in Atlanta, a motivation and training professional association with a client list that includes Xerox Corporation, General Electric, and AT&T. She is also the national president of The Links, Inc.

George Herman ("Babe") Ruth (130), 1895–1948, played professional baseball for the New York Yankees from 1920 to 1935. He held the record for the most career home runs for nearly forty years until Hank Aaron broke it in 1974. He was the American League's Most Valuable Player in 1923.

S

John Salley (130) played on three NBA championship teams, two with the Detroit Pistons and one with the Chicago Bulls.

Deion Sanders (131) plays both professional baseball (the Cincinnati Reds) and football (the Dallas Cowboys). Sanders also has the distinction of winning back-to-back Super Bowl rings with two different football teams, the San Francisco 49ers and the Dallas Cowboys.

Leonard Sanders (132), a retired mine worker in the small town of Elkville, Illinois, won a $20 million lottery jackpot. Sanders divided up the money with his family and used some of it to build and equip a recreation center for people over age fifty.

Catherine Schaller (52) is a Chicago public school teacher and the 1996 recipient of the Milken Family Foundation National Educator Award. Schaller links her students' academic work to real life by having them manage a Get Real Gift Center store. Her students also work weekly retail jobs and save money in a school bank.

Patricia ("Pat") Schroeder (134) is president of the American Association of Publishers (AAP) and a former member of the U.S. House of Representatives from Colorado.

Matthew S. Scott (134) is a senior editor of *Black Enterprise*, a magazine that encourages and supports black business aspirations.

Abdulalim Shabazz (53, 100) has been heralded for his unusual success in teaching mathematics. He chairs the Clark Atlanta University mathematics department.

Diane Shelton (116) is the CEO of West Love, a fashion boutique in Culver City, California.

Linda Shepard (3, 87) is a program manager of Women Employed Career Links, a mentoring program for teenage girls in Chicago.

Jim Shifflett (9) is the owner of Vortech Systems, a home-based computer company that produces documentaries and film special effects.

Robert Shillman (89, 130) is the founder and CEO of the Cognex Corporation in Natick, Massachusetts, a company involved in *machine vision,* a high-tech process that enables computers to "see."

Sierra Leone proverb (38) Sierra Leone is a country on the west coast of Africa.

Naomi Sims (91) is founder and chair of Naomi Sims Beauty Products, Inc. She was formerly a highly successful fashion model.

Sinbad (90) (né David Adkins) is a successful comedian and actor who starred in the television series *A Different World* and had his own television specials, *All the Way Live* and *Brain Damaged.* He also has film credits: *The Meteor Man, Houseguest,* and *First Kid.*

John Singleton (133) received three writing awards while a student at the University of Southern California film school and was nominated for an Academy Award for Best Director for his first movie *Boyz in the 'Hood.* He also wrote and directed *Poetic Justice* and *Higher Learning.*

Courtney Sloane (72) owns the Alternative Design company in Jersey City, New Jersey. The business specializes in interior design and furnishings. Her clients include Queen Latifah, MTV host Bill Bellamy, and *Vibe* magazine.

Ken Smikle (63) is the president of a Chicago-based research firm, which specializes in tracking African American consumers and marketing. The firm publishes *Target Market News.*

Barbara Smith (14, 27, 33, 82) is the founding partner of B.Smith's restaurants, located in New York City and Washington, D.C. She is also a former fashion model.

Joshua I. Smith (120) is the owner and CEO of MAXIMA Corporation, a computer information-management company based in Lanham, Maryland.

Steve Smith (140) is a starting guard for the Atlanta Hawks professional basketball team, who donated $2.5 million to his alma mater, Michigan State University, to fund scholarships and an academic center for student athletes.

Buster Soaries, Jr. (65), is a Baptist minister and president and CEO of PROCLAIM, a gospel recording label.

Pervis Spann (30, 133), "the blues man," is a radio personality and entertainment promoter who has put on thousands of shows. He is president of WVON radio station in Chicago.

Shelby Steele (67) is a research fellow at the Hoover Institute, a think tank at Stanford University in California. He has also been a professor of English at San Jose State University and has written for *The American Scholar, The Washington Post, The New Republic,* and *The New York Times Book Review.* In 1989, he won a National Magazine Award. Steele is the author of *The Content of Our Character.*

Brian Steinberg (135) is a writer based in Washington, D.C., who contributes to *Entrepreneur,* a magazine for small businesses.

Brooke Stephens (93) is a financial consultant in New York City and the author of *Talking Dollars and Making Sense.*

Bill Stephney (62, 64) owns Music in Cinema, a company that produces songs and sound tracks for feature films.

Michelle Stevens (2) is the night news editor of *The Chicago Sun-Times.*

George Subira (80, 110, 122) published a series of books in the 1980s that were the first guides to income enhancement and money management written specifically for African Americans. His titles are *Black Folks' Guide to Making Big Money in America, Black Folks' Guide to Business Success,* and *Getting Black Folks to Sell.* Subira is a former professor at Seton Hall University.

Wardell Sullivan (122) owns Sullivan & Associates, Inc., a training/consulting firm in Indianapolis, used by both not-for-profit and profit concerns, including Allstate Insurance, Dow-Elanco, and Thompson Consumer Electronics.

Barry Suskind (135) founded International Technologies & Finance, a New York City firm that has raised some $600 million for emerging companies.

Darnell Sutton (89) is president and co-owner of Sutton Galleries furniture showroom in Rockville, Maryland. Sutton also spends time talking to inner-city youths, encouraging them to become entrepreneurs.

Percy Sutton (100) is cofounder (in 1972, with Clarence Jones) and board chair of Inner City Broadcasting in New York City.

Swahili proverb (39) Swahili is a "trade" language spoken primarily in the southeastern part of the African continent.

T

Joanna Tamer (30, 83, 87) is president of S.O.S., Inc., a consulting firm in Los Angeles for new media developers, publishers, distributors, and retailers. Her clients include Blockbuster Video, HarperCollins book publishers, and Time-Life, Inc.

Don Tapscott (30, 34, 41, 50, 51, 128) chairs the Toronto-based Alliance for Converging Technologies, a think tank investigating new media's impact on business. He also authored *The Digital Economy.*

Susan L. Taylor (4, 40, 68, 73, 115) is editor-in-chief of *Essence* magazine and senior vice president of Essence Communications. Before joining *Essence,* she founded and successfully operated her own cosmetic company, supplying beauty products to African American women.

Terence (19, 32, 40, 46, 86) (Publius Terentius Afer), 190–159 B.C., was a slave from Carthage (in ancient northern Africa), who achieved fame as a poet and playwright in Rome.

Roy Terry (136) is co-owner (with his brother Rudolph) of an apparel-making business, Terry Manufacturing Company, in Roanoke, Alabama.

Debi Thomas (18, 99) was the first woman of African descent to win the U.S. Figure Skating Title in 1986, and she won the World Figure Skating Title the same year. In 1988, she won the U.S. title again and took the bronze medal at the Olympics. Thomas is currently studying medicine.

Henry David Thoreau (92), 1817–1862, was an influential writer who lived in Concord, Massachusetts. Thoreau authored *Walden, or Life in the Woods* and *Civil Disobedience.*

Howard Thurman (86), 1900–1981, founded the Church for the Fellowship of All Peoples in 1944. This nondenominational church allowed Thurman to utilize some creative, nontraditional worship practices, including ministering to a racially mixed congregation. He published a number of poetic meditations, including *Jesus and the Disinherited, The Inward Journey,* and *The Luminous Darkness.*

Tibetan proverb (6) Tibet is a country in central Asia located between India and China.

Isaac Tigrett (138) founded the House of Blues, a national chain of nightclubs. He also cofounded the Hard Rock Cafe chain of restaurants, which he sold for $108 million in 1988.

Johnnie Tillmon-Blackston (70) is the founding chair of the National Welfare Rights Organization.

Alexander Torimiro (104) is a former chemical engineer from Cameroon, who now owns The Torimiro Corporation, producers of Victoria Tea in Ontario, Canada. He opened a manufacturing facility in Harlem, which employs 120 people.

Brian Tracy (3, 51, 82, 88, 121, 122), an entrepreneur who has built a multimillion-dollar seminar and consulting business, is the author of *Advanced Selling Strategies.*

Dempsey J. Travis (85, 125) is the president and CEO of Travis Realty Company in Chicago and the author of several books, including *Harold, the People's Mayor; I Refuse to Learn to Fail; Don't Stop Me Now;* and *Real Estate Is the Gold in Your Future.*

John Tu (138) and David Sun, both immigrants from Taiwan, cofounded Kingston Technology Corporation in Fountain Valley, California, the world's top maker of computer-memory products. The owners generously share all profits with employees.

R. Edward ("Ted") Turner (140) founded Turner Television, pioneer in the all-news format with Cable News Network (CNN). Turner merged his enterprises with Time-Warner, Inc., of which he is now vice chair.

Mike Tyson (84) is a former world heavyweight boxing champion. He has won forty-five of his forty-eight bouts and earned more than $150 million from his last eight fights.

V

Mike Vance (33) chairs the Creative Thinking Association of America.

Melvin Van Peebles (10, 97) is a man of many talents. He has been an options trader on Wall Street; written *Bold Money* and *Panther;* produced and directed *Sweet Sweetback's Baadasss Song, Panther,* and *Watermelon Man;* and acted in the films *Posse* and *Boomerang.*

Iyanla Vanzant (2) has overcome a number of obstacles to become a Yoruba priestess, inspirational speaker, and best-selling author of *Tapping the Power Within, Acts of Faith, Value in the Valley, Faith in the Valley,* and *Spirit of a Man.*

Roger von Oech (34, 35) wrote the book *A Whack on the Side of the Head.*

W

Alice Walker (11, 15) is the cofounder and publisher of Wild Trees Press and an award-winning writer. She received the Pulitzer Prize and the American Book Award for her novel *The Color Purple*. Walker also writes poetry (her poetry books include *Goodnight Willie Lee, I'll See You in the Morning*, and *Horses Make the Landscape Look More Beautiful*) and essays *(In Search of Our Mothers' Gardens* and *Living by the Word)*.

Madame C. J. Walker (28, 114, 138) (née Sarah Breedlove), 1867–1919, was the first member of her family to be born outside slavery and began her work life doing laundry. Walker went on to create, develop, and manufacture hair-care products and to build her own factory. She trained women to sell her products and became the first female self-made millionaire in the United States.

Maggie Lena Walker (73), 1865–1934, began her career as a public-school teacher then went on to work for a bank and eventually founded the St. Luke Penny Savings Bank in Richmond, Virginia.

Margaret Walker (see Margaret Walker Alexander)

Samuel Moore ("Sam") Walton (23, 128, 131), 1918–1992, founded the Wal-Mart chain of retail stores. His autobiography is titled *Sam Walton Made in America: My Story*.

Rita Warford (2) is a self-employed Chicago jazz vocalist.

Ralph Warner (114, 125) is the cofounder and owner of Nolo Press in Berkeley, California.

Claudette Warner-Milne (9, 45) used her love of sewing to start her own business, Make Mine Leather, after she lost her job. She made hand-crafted leather accessories and sold them from her home in Silver Spring, Maryland.

Booker T. Washington (28, 114), 1856–1915, was born into slavery but determinedly educated himself after he was freed. He was the founder and first president of Tuskegee Institute in Alabama. Washington was a confidant of U.S. presidents Theodore Roosevelt and William Howard Taft.

Denzel Washington (44, 108) made his movie debut in 1981 in *Carbon Copy*. He has gone on to star in *A Soldier's Story, Mo' Better Blues, The Pelican Brief, Devil in a Blue Dress,* and many other films. Washington was nominated for an Academy Award for *Cry Freedom*; he won the Oscar for Best Supporting Actor in *Glory* and the New York Film Critics Award for the title role in *Malcolm X*.

Harold Washington (91), 1922–1987, began his elective political career in the Illinois legislature, represented Chicago in the U.S. Congress, and in 1983 became the first African American mayor of Chicago.

Maxine Waters (91, 100) was elected to the California State Assembly in 1976 and served as the majority whip there. She is now a representative from California to the U.S. Congress.

Ron Watkins (31, 119, 140) is chair of the Heritage International Trade Association in Chicago, author of *Doing Business in Africa: Myths and Realities,* and writer of the *Afrique* column "Thinking Globally."

Renita Jo Weems (5, 38) is a professor of Old Testament studies in the divinity school at Vanderbilt University in Nashville, Tennessee. Weems also authored *Just a Sister Away* and *I Asked for Intimacy*.

Dorothy West (1) is the last surviving member of the Harlem Renaissance. Her first novel, *The Living Is Easy,* was initially published in 1948 and her most recent, *The Wedding,* in 1995.

Byron P. White (63) is a staff writer for the *Chicago Tribune*.

Dorothy J. White (123) owns Miracle Services, Inc., a full-service janitorial business in Hanover, Maryland.

Richard C. Whiteley (126) is a business consultant and president of the Forum Corporation in Boston.

John Edgar Wideman (87) was a Rhodes Scholar in 1968 and has won the PEN/Faulkner Award two times. He is an English professor and prolific writer whose published works include *Brothers and Keepers, Fatheralong, A Glance Away, Sent for You Yesterday, Philadelphia Fire,* and many others.

Bob Wilburn (65) is president of the Park Manor Ministry, Million Man March Bus #7 in Chicago. Wilburn and the other men from Bus #7 have developed a program to mentor students at an elementary school near the Altgeld Gardens housing project.

L. Douglas ("Doug") Wilder (30) was the first African American to be elected a state governor, in Virginia in 1989.

Terrie Williams (3, 21, 23, 55, 70, 76, 91, 103, 105, 108, 117, 122, 128) owns and operates a top New York public-relations agency that handles such clients as Eddie Murphy, Janet Jackson, 20th Century Fox, AT&T, and HBO, among others. She is also the author of *The Personal Touch*.

Vanessa Williams (92) began her musical career in 1989 with her album *The Right Stuff*. She has won the NAACP Image Award two times and a number of Grammys. Her album *The Comfort Zone* attained double-platinum status. She is also an actress who has appeared in film, on television, and on Broadway in the title role in *Kiss of the Spider Woman*.

William Willimon (14) is a professor at Duke University and co-author (with Rolf Osterberg and Thomas H. Naylor) of *The Search for Meaning in the Workplace*.

Oprah Winfrey (75, 80, 86, 131, 139) hosts and owns *The Oprah Winfrey Show*, which is produced in her Harpo Studios. Winfrey was named Broadcaster of the Year in 1988 and was nominated for an Academy Award for *The Color Purple*. She has also produced television movies, such as *Brewster Place* and *There Are No Children Here*, and has won many Emmy awards.

George C. Wolfe (86) created, produced, and directed the popular show *Bring in 'Da Noise, Bring in 'Da Funk*. Wolfe also directed *Angels in America* and runs the New York Shakespeare Festival. He authored *The Colored Museum*.

Eldrick "Tiger" Woods (19, 44, 94) at age twenty-one became the youngest person to win a Masters championship. He won the Masters golf tournament at Augusta National in his first attempt with a record four-round score of 270 and a record twelve-shot margin of victory. Woods, incredibly, won four tournaments in his first seven and a half months of professional competition. He had also won three-straight amateur titles before turning professional in 1996.

James M. Woods, Sr. (29), is the owner of Woods Industries, which manufactures parts for aircraft and automobiles in Los

Angeles, and cofounder of the Kedren Community Health Centers.

Carter G. Woodson (47), 1875–1950, was a historian, educator, and author of *The Miseducation of the Negro.* Woodson was a founder of Negro History Week—now Black History Month—and the Association for the Study of Afro-American Life and History.

Anne Wortham (62) is a sociologist at Washington and Lee University and a continuing visiting scholar at the Hoover Institution, a think tank at Stanford University in California.

Richard Wright (4, 16), 1908–1960, had a major influence on a number of other prominent writers with his first novel, *Native Son.* He also authored *Black Boy; Uncle Tom's Children; White Man, Listen!;* and several other books.

X

Malcolm X (El Hajj Malik El-Shabazz) (86), 1926–1965, educated himself in prison, where he joined the Nation of Islam. As the national spokesperson for the Nation, Malcolm received much media attention and continues to be widely admired, particularly among African Americans. His publications include *The Autobiography of Malcolm X, Malcolm X Speaks, Malcolm X at Harvard,* and others.

Y

Andrew Young (1, 13, 17, 37, 54, 131) is a former ambassador to the United Nations, representative to the U.S. Congress from Atlanta, and mayor of Atlanta. Young became widely known for his work with Martin Luther King, Jr., in the civil-rights movement. He is an advocate and supporter of entrepreneurship and was cochair of the Atlanta Committee for the 1996 Olympic Games. He is the author of *An Easy Burden.*

Whitney Moore Young, Jr. (29), 1921–1971, was named executive director of the National Urban League in 1961 and served there until his death. He was the author of *To Be Equal*.

Z

Jack Zenger (21, 35) chairs Times Mirror Training, Inc., the world's largest group of employee training companies, including Zenger Miller and Learning International. He is the author of several books, including *Not Just for CEOs*.

Andrew Zenoff (133) is the founder and owner of Zenoff Products, manufacturers of My Brest-Friend, a support pillow for anyone feeding a baby. The company was started in 1995.

Credits

About the Author

Janet Cheatham Bell is a writer and publishing consultant living in Chicago. She has been a senior editor of literature textbooks for Ginn & Company (now Silver-Burdett & Ginn), a consultant to Baker & Taylor Books, and associate editor of *The Black Scholar.* She was also a curriculum consultant for the Indiana Department of Education and taught writing and African-American literature at several colleges and universities.

Bell was named one of "The Lit 50, Chicago's Book World: Who Really Counts" in 1995 and 1996 by *New City.* She is a member of the Society of Midland Authors.